LifeChange

A NAVPRESS BIBLE STUDY SERIES

A life-changing
encounter with God's Word

JOB

Suffering is a mystery—
an invitation to explore and to listen.

NAVPRESS

A NavPress resource published in alliance
with Tyndale House Publishers, Inc.

NAVPRESS⬤

NavPress is the publishing ministry of The Navigators, an international Christian organization and leader in personal spiritual development. NavPress is committed to helping people grow spiritually and enjoy lives of meaning and hope through personal and group resources that are biblically rooted, culturally relevant, and highly practical.

For more information, visit www.NavPress.com.

24 23 22 21 20 19 18
12 11 10 9   8   7   6

CONTENTS

HOW TO USE THIS STUDY

Objectives

Most guides in the LIFECHANGE series of Bible studies cover one book of the Bible. Although the LIFECHANGE guides vary with the books they explore, they share some common goals.

1. To provide you with a firm foundation of understanding and a thirst to return to the book.

2. To teach you by example how to study a book of the Bible without structured guides.

3. To give you all the historical background, word definitions, and explanatory notes you need, so that your only other reference is the Bible.

4. To help you grasp the message of the book as a whole.

5. To teach you how to let God's Word transform you into Christ's image.

Each lesson in this study is designed to take 60 to 90 minutes to complete on your own. The guide is based on the assumption that you are completing one lesson per week, but if time is limited you can do half a lesson per week or whatever amount allows you to be thorough.

Flexibility

LIFECHANGE guides are flexible, allowing you to adjust the quantity and depth of your study to meet your individual needs. The guide offers many optional questions in addition to the regular numbered questions. The optional questions, which appear in the margins of the study pages, include the following:

Optional Application. Nearly all application questions are optional; we hope you will do as many as you can without overcommitting yourself.

For Thought and Discussion. Beginning Bible students should be able to handle these, but even advanced students need to think about them. These questions frequently deal with ethical issues and other biblical principles.

They often offer cross-references to spark thought, but the references do not give obvious answers. They are good for group discussions.

For Further Study. These include: (a) cross-references that shed light on a topic the book discusses, and (b) questions that delve deeper into the passage. You can omit them to shorten a lesson without missing a major point of the passage.

If you are meeting in a group, decide together which optional questions to prepare for each lesson, and how much of the lesson you will cover at the next meeting. Normally, the group leader should make this decision, but you might let each member choose his or her own application questions.

As you grow in your walk with God, you will find the LifeChange guide growing with you—a helpful reference on a topic, a continuing challenge for application, a source of questions for many levels of growth.

Overview and details

The study begins with an introduction to the book of Job. The key to interpretation is context—what is the whole passage or book *about*?—and the key to context is purpose—what is the author's *aim* for the whole work? In lesson 1, you will lay the foundation for your study of Job by asking yourself, *Why did the author (and God) write the book? What did they want to accomplish? What is the book about?*

In lessons 2 through 13, you will analyze successive passages of Job in detail. You will cover the dialogue (3:1–37:24) topically rather than passage by passage because the debaters jump from point to point, and the thoughts are easier to follow if arranged by topic.

In lesson 13, you will review Job, returning to the big picture to see whether your view of it has changed after closer study. Review will also strengthen your grasp of major issues and give you an idea of how you have grown from your study.

Kinds of questions

Bible study on your own—without a structured guide—follows a progression. First you observe: What does the passage *say*? Then you interpret: What does the passage *mean*? Lastly you apply: How does this truth *affect* my life?

Some of the "how" and "why" questions will take some creative thinking, even prayer, to answer. Some are opinion questions without clearcut right answers; these will lend themselves to discussions and side studies.

Don't let your study become an exercise in knowledge alone. Treat the passages as God's Word, and stay in dialogue with Him as you study. Pray, "Lord, what do You want me to see here?" "Father, why is this true?" "Lord, how does this apply to my life?"

It is important that you write down your answers. The act of writing clarifies your thinking and helps you to remember.

Study aids

A list of reference materials, including a few notes of explanation to help you make good use of them, begins on page 123. This guide is designed to include enough background to let you interpret with just your Bible and the guide. Still, if you want more information on a subject or want to study a book on your own, try the references listed.

Scripture versions

Unless otherwise indicated, the Bible quotations in this guide are from the New International Version of the Bible. Other versions cited are the Revised Standard Version (RSV), the New American Standard Bible (NASB), and the King James Version (KJV).

Use any translation you like for study, preferably more than one. A paraphrase such as *The Living Bible* is not accurate enough for study, but it can be helpful for comparison or devotional reading.

Memorizing and meditating

A psalmist wrote, "I have hidden your word in my heart that I might not sin against you" (Psalm 119:11). If you write down a verse or passage that challenges or encourages you, and reflect on it often for a week or more, you will find it beginning to affect your motives and actions. We forget quickly what we read once; we remember what we ponder.

When you find a significant verse or passage, you might copy it onto a card to keep with you. Set aside five minutes during each day just to think about what the passage might mean in your life. Recite it over to yourself, exploring its meaning. Then, return to your passage as often as you can during your day, for a brief review. You will soon find it coming to mind spontaneously.

For group study

A group of four to ten people allows the richest discussions, but you can adapt this guide for other sized groups. It will suit a wide range of group types, such as home Bible studies, growth groups, youth groups, and business-men's studies. Both new and experienced Bible students, and new and mature Christians, will benefit from the guide. You can omit or leave for later years any questions you find too easy or too hard.

The guide is intended to lead a group through one lesson per week. However, feel free to split lessons if you want to discuss them more thoroughly. Or, omit some questions in a lesson if preparation or discussion time is limited. You can always return to this guide for personal study later. You will be able to discuss only a few questions at length, so choose some for discussion and others for background. Make time at each discussion for members to ask about anything they didn't understand.

Each lesson in the guide ends with a section called "For the group." These sections give advice on how to focus a discussion, how you might apply the lesson in your group, how you might shorten a lesson, and so on. The group leader should read each "For the group" at least a week ahead so that he or she can tell the group how to prepare for the next lesson.

Each member should prepare for a meeting by writing answers for all of the background and discussion questions to be covered. If the group decides not to take an hour per week for private preparation, then expect to take at least two meetings per lesson to work through the questions. Application will be very difficult, however, without private thought and prayer.

Two reasons for studying in a group are accountability and support. When each member commits in front of the rest to seek growth in an area of life, you can pray with one another, listen jointly for God's guidance, help one another to resist temptation, assure each other that the other's growth matters to you, use the group to practice spiritual principles, and so on. Pray about one another's commitments and needs at most meetings. Spend the first few minutes of each meeting sharing any results from applications prompted by previous lessons. Then discuss new applications toward the end of the meeting. Follow such sharing with prayer for these and other needs.

If you write down each other's applications and prayer requests, you are more likely to remember to pray for them during the week, ask about them at the next meeting, and notice answered prayers. You might want to get a notebook for prayer requests and discussion notes.

Notes taken during discussion will help you to remember, follow up on ideas, stay on the subject, and clarify a total view of an issue. But don't let note-taking keep you from participating. Some groups choose one member at each meeting to take notes. Then someone copies the notes and distributes them at the next meeting. Rotating these tasks can help include people. Some groups have someone take notes on a large pad of paper or erasable marker board (pre-formed shower wallboard works well), so that everyone can see what has been recorded.

Pages 125–126 list some good sources of counsel for leading group studies.

Lesson One

INTRODUCTION

Job and God

Map of the Near East

Brothers and sisters, as an example of patience in the face of suffering, take the prophets who spoke in the name of the Lord. As you know, we count as blessed those who have persevered. You have heard of Job's perseverance and have seen what the Lord finally brought about. The Lord is full of compassion and mercy.

(James 5:10-11)

"The patience of Job" is proverbial, but in fact Job wasn't patient. The Greek word in James 5:11 praises Job's perseverance, and that is what he was: loudly, emotionally, impatiently perseverant in the face of suffering that would drive

9

most people to despair. In one man's story, the relationship between man and God is explored profoundly.

The Story

The plot is simple: Job is a good man overwhelmed by sudden calamities. He doesn't know why; only the reader knows what is happening in heaven. Three friends visit Job to comfort him, and the four heatedly debate why Job has been so afflicted. Failing to persuade Job, the friends finally fall silent. Job still insists his suffering is unjust and demands redress from God. Then a young man named Elihu appears, claiming to have the ultimate answer for Job but adding few new insights. At last the Lord Himself appears. He asks Job a long series of questions. This response changes Job's attitude, and he repents of his rash words about God. In the end, the Lord rebukes Job's friends and praises Job, and He restores to Job double what he lost.

A simple plot, but in the course of it the author deals with such questions as:

What is God like? Is He really perfectly good, just, and sovereign as the Scriptures tell us?

What is man in God's eyes? Is he a worm or a prized work of art? An enemy, a friend, or a pawn?

What does God expect of man? What is "righteousness"? How should a person relate to God?

What is faith? Can a person doubt and question God, and still have faith?

Why do people suffer? Is suffering always punishment for sin? Does God let innocent people suffer, and if so, why?

Why do people obey God? Do they do it only to gain rewards and blessings? Would anyone keep worshipping God if there were no tangible benefits?

How can someone help a friend who is suffering? What are some of the right and wrong things to say?

Questions like these are as relevant now as they were three thousand years ago.

Difficulties

As relevant as it is, Job is not an easy book for modern readers. First of all, it is written mostly in poetry, and Hebrew poetry is different from what most of us are used to reading. Second, it is full of words that occur rarely or never in the rest of the Old Testament and phrases that baffle even experts. A quick comparison of several translations reveals that translators have often come to varied views of what a given verse means. Some versions, such as the Jerusalem

Bible and New English Bible, follow a theory that the only way to make sense of Job is to move verses around (putting 24:6 before 24:3, for instance). These difficulties don't mean that non-experts in Hebrew can't study Job; they mean only that we will get more out of the book if we do several things:

First, whenever possible, compare at least two translations. For example, the KJV, NASB, and RSV attempt to be literal, so they are often unintelligible when the original is obscure. The NIV and TEV try to be intelligible, so they often paraphrase or make an educated guess when rendering a difficult verse.

Second, know at least the basic rules of Hebrew poetry. The Study Skill on pages 39–40 deals with that.

Third, understand what *wisdom* is in Hebrew tradition. Job is a book about wisdom, as are Proverbs and Ecclesiastes. (We will discuss wisdom shortly.)

Fourth, pay attention to the *context* — the overall gist of each verse. What are the whole passage, the whole chapter, and the whole book getting at? Remember that in the end, God rebukes Job's friends for their words — does this mean that what they say is always true, sometimes true, or always false? God praises Job — does this mean that what he says is always true, sometimes true, or always false? Passages from other books of Scripture can sometimes help us decide what is true and what is false. For practice in this kind of discernment, you might look at the following verses describing God. The first pair are Job's words, and the second are the words of one of his friends.

Job: "Even if I summoned him and he responded, I do not believe he would give me a hearing. He would crush me with a storm and multiply my wounds for no reason" (9:16-17).

"But he stands alone, and who can oppose him? He does whatever he pleases" (23:13).

Eliphaz: "Can a mortal be more righteous than God? Can even a strong man be more pure than his Maker?" (4:17).

"What pleasure would it give the Almighty if you were righteous? What would he gain if your ways were blameless?" (22:3).

Because translations of Job differ so much, we have given few explanations of individual verses. If you need more help, consult a commentary (see page 123 for some suggestions).

Wisdom

Basically, "Wisdom is the discipline of applying truth to one's life in the light of experience."[1] Wisdom is meant to be not theoretical and abstract but practical and personal. It should teach a person to live responsibly and successfully by learning from his own and elders' experience.

In most developed nations of the ancient Near East, there was a class of wise men and women devoted to gaining and teaching wisdom. In Israel, at least by the time David became king (1010 BC), they became important as the teachers and counselors. A parent would send a child to a wisdom teacher, and the wise man or woman would act as parent to the pupil (in Proverbs, for instance, the teacher addresses "my child"). Of course, most parents taught their own children at home, but anyone with enough money wanted a proper wise man for his son.[2]

Wise men liked to arrive at truth and edify an audience by debating some principle for living. However, the contest was not like a modern debate, where the speakers try to find flaws in their opponents' facts and logic and to support their own deductions. Instead, the winner of the ancient debate was the one with the most "brilliant rhetoric."[3] When you read the debate in Job 3–37, you might feel that the men jump from point to point, repeat themselves, ignore each other's statements until chapters later, and generally talk past each other. However, the result is brilliant and moving poetry. This is the style of an ancient debate.

One of the basic tenets of wisdom was that God punishes the wicked and blesses the righteous. The wise came to regard this not as a general principle but as an absolute law. There was no such thing as an innocent person suffering. Therefore, everybody knew that the prosperous people in town were the godly ones, and the poor and afflicted were impious. This was justice, and because God was just, could He ever fail to obey this law? "No" was the firm response of the wise. But the author of Job, himself steeped in the wisdom tradition, had some radical views on this subject.

The structure of Job

At first glance in English, it looks as though most of Job is in poetry, except for a prologue and epilogue (see 1:1–2:13; 42:7-17) in prose. Recently, however, scholars have been realizing that Old Testament (and other ancient) writers often put narrative in prose and speeches in poetry. This is true throughout the book of Ruth, and so it is in Job. The speeches in the prologue and epilogue are in poetry just like the dialogue; what makes Job unique is that it is mostly speeches.[4] Some understanding of Hebrew poetry is a great help in interpreting Job. If you are interested, read the box on pages 39–40.

Prologue–body–epilogue was a common ancient form because people liked balance. We also find that two tests of Job (see 1:6–2:10) balance two speeches by God (see 38:1–41:34); the dialogue runs in three cycles with introduction and conclusion (see 3:1–27:23); and Job's summary counterweights Elihu's (see 29:1–37:24). The outline on pages 14–15 reflects this analysis.

Author and date

Scholars always want to know who wrote a book and when. For Job we just don't know. Some experts think the book went through several revisions before the current version with the Holy Spirit's seal of authority was produced. Others think one person wrote it, perhaps over several decades.

Dates from the time of Moses to 200 BC have been proposed. Details in the prologue (where Job is his family's priest and his wealth is based on animals) suggest that Job lived in the age of the patriarchs (about 2500 to 1500 BC). Most scholars now date the writing of the book somewhere between Solomon's reign and the exile to Babylon (970–586 BC). Those were the years of wisdom's greatest glory in Israel, so a book that debates the true nature of wisdom seems natural at that time.

First impressions

Most LifeChange studies guide you through a book chapter by chapter, but this one is different. The debate doesn't unfold each side's argument step-by-step; instead, the speakers repeat themselves, digress, respond to a point made five chapters earlier, and so on. Therefore, to help you get a clear overview of forty-two chapters in just thirteen lessons, we've organized the study topically. You'll examine what everyone says about God's power in one lesson and man's nature in another so you can draw your own conclusions on each subject. The prologue, the interlude in chapter 28, God's two speeches, and the epilogue each make sense on their own, so lessons 2, 10, 11, 12, and 13 deal with these.

Many questions list several references from Job so as to give you as full a view of the book as possible. If your time is limited, you can skip some references in each question. If you feel that the selected references are too restrictive and force you to certain conclusions, you can read larger passages and make up your own mind.

Because the study doesn't cover 3:1–27:23 and 29:1–37:24 chapter by chapter, you should read as much of the book as possible before beginning lesson 2. Read at least chapters 1 through 6 and 38 through 42, and leaf through the rest of the book with the outline on pages 14–15 as a guide. If you take even an hour to skim the book and see what goes on in each chapter, you'll find it much easier later to organize and remember what you learn. Also, you'll get a taste of the poetry of Job, which is grand even in translation. It brings alive what can be just an old dry adage:

The fear of the Lord—that is wisdom,
and to shun evil is understanding. (Job 28:28)

As you read, jot here your first impressions of the book, questions you'd like answered as you study more deeply, how the story makes you feel, and so on.

_____

_____

_____

_____

_____

_____

_____

_____

_____

_____

_____

_____

_____

_____

_____

_____

_____

_____

_____

_____

_____

_____

_____

Outline of Job[5]

I. Prologue: Job Tested (1:1–2:13)
  A. Job's integrity (1:1-5)
  B. The first test (1:6-22)
    1. The first assembly (1:6-12)
    2. The first disasters (1:13-19)
    3. Job's first reaction (1:20-22)
  C. The second test (2:1-10)
    1. The second assembly (2:1-7a)
    2. Job's illness (2:7b-8)
    3. Job's second reaction (2:9-10)
  D. Job's friends arrive (2:11-13)

II. Dialogue Between Job and His Friends (3:1–27:23)
    A. Job's lamentation (3:1-26)
    B. First round of speeches (4:1–14:22)
       1. Eliphaz (4:1–5:27)
       2. Job (6:1–7:21)
       3. Bildad (8:1-22)
       4. Job (9:1–10:22)
       5. Zophar (11:1-20)
       6. Job (12:1–14:22)
    C. Second round of speeches (15:1–21:34)
       1. Eliphaz (15:1-35)
       2. Job (16:1–17:16)
       3. Bildad (18:1-21)
       4. Job (19:1-29)
       5. Zophar (20:1-29)
       6. Job (21:1-34)
    D. Third round of speeches (22:1–26:14)
       1. Eliphaz (22:1-30)
       2. Job (23:1–24:25)
       3. Bildad (25:1-6)
       4. Job (26:1-14)
    E. Job's conclusion (27:1-23)

III. Interlude on Wisdom (28:1-28)

IV. Monologues: Job and Elihu (29:1–37:24)
    A. Job summarizes his case (29:1–31:40)
       1. Job's past honor and blessing (29:1-25)
       2. Job's present humiliation and suffering (30:1-31)
       3. Job's ultimate appeal and oath (31:1-40)
    B. Elihu states the human verdict (32:1–37:24)
       1. Introduction (32:1-5)
       2. Elihu's first speech (32:6–33:33)
       3. Elihu's second speech (34:1-37)
       4. Elihu's third speech (35:1-16)
       5. Elihu's fourth speech (36:1–37:24)

V. The Lord and Job (38:1–42:6)
    A. First round (38:1–40:5)
       1. The Lord (38:1–40:2)
       2. Job (40:3-5)
    B. Second round (40:6–42:6)
       1. The Lord (40:6–41:34)
       2. Job (42:1-6)

VI. Epilogue: The Outcome of the Test (42:7-17)
    A. The Lord states the divine verdict (42:7-9)
    B. Job restored (42:10-17)

For the group

This "For the group" section and the ones in later lessons are intended to suggest ways of structuring your discussions. Feel free to select what suits your group. The main goals of this lesson are to get to know the book of Job as a whole and the people with whom you are going to study it.

Worship. Some groups like to begin with prayer and/or singing. Some share requests for prayer at the beginning but leave the actual prayer until after the study. Others prefer just to chat and have refreshments for a while, then open the study with a brief prayer for the Holy Spirit's guidance and leave worship and prayer until the end.

Warm-up. The beginning of a new study is a good time to lay a foundation for honest sharing of ideas, to get comfortable with each other, and to encourage a sense of common purpose. One way to establish common ground is to talk about what each person hopes to get out of your study of Job and out of any prayer, singing, sharing, outreach, or anything else you might do together. You can also share what you hope to give as well as get. If you have someone write down each member's hopes and expectations, then you can look back at these goals later to see if they are being met. Goal setting at the beginning can also help you avoid confusion when one person thinks the main point of the group is to learn the Scripture, while another thinks it is to support each other in daily Christian life, and another thinks prayer or outreach is the chief business.

Introduction. Ideally, everyone should have read the whole book of Job before you meet together. However, probably few people will have done this because Job is long and difficult for those who don't often read poetry. Therefore, the introduction is meant to give you some basic background to make studying the book easier. To make sure everyone begins lesson 2 understanding the introduction, ask some questions about it, such as these:

> What is the plot of Job? (Have someone tell the story briefly.)
> What kinds of questions do the characters discuss in the dialogue? (You might discuss which of the questions are most interesting to group members. This information may help you guide the discussion later.)
> What is wisdom? How is the book of Job part of the wisdom tradition?
> How is the dialogue in Job different from a modern debate?
> When you read chapters 1 through 6 and 38 through 42, what first impressions, questions, and so on did you come up with? (Someone in the group should write the questions down so the whole group can keep them in mind during future sessions.)
> Did anyone read about Hebrew poetry on pages 39–40? What are the main things we should understand about it before we start studying Job?
> Is everything Job says true? Is everything he says false? How can you tell? Why is this important to remember?

How to Use This Study. Advise group members to read the "How to Use This Study" section on pages 5–8 if they have not already done so. You might go over important points that you think the group should especially notice. For example, point out the optional questions in the margins. These are available as group discussion questions, ideas for application, and suggestions for further study. It is unlikely that anyone will have the time or desire to answer all the optional questions and do all the applications. A person might do one "Optional Application" for any given lesson. You might choose one or two "For Thought and Discussion" questions for your group discussion, or you might spend all your time on the numbered questions. If someone wants to write answers to the optional questions, suggest that he use the margins or a separate notebook. It will also be helpful for discussion notes, prayer requests, answers to prayers, application plans, and so on. State clearly from the beginning how much time you expect group members to commit both for preparation and group meetings. Agree to be faithful about starting and ending meetings on time unless the group agrees to do otherwise.

Invite everyone to ask questions about the introduction or the "How to Use This Study" section.

Wrap-up. The group leader should have read through lesson 2 and its "For the group" section so that he or she can briefly tell the group what to expect in the lesson. Whet everyone's appetite by asking the group to think about any optional questions that you plan to discuss. For example, if you want the group to focus on what God does in 1:1–2:13 and why, you might suggest that members think about the "For Thought and Discussion" questions that deal with that issue.

Worship. Many groups like to end with singing and/or prayer. This can include songs or prayers that respond to what you've learned in Bible study, or prayers for specific needs of group members. Some people are shy about sharing personal needs or praying aloud in groups, especially before they know the other people well. If this is true of your group, then a song and/or some silent prayer and a short closing prayer spoken by the leader might be an appropriate ending.

1. Gordon D. Fee and Douglas Stuart, *How to Read the Bible for All Its Worth* (Grand Rapids, MI: Zondervan, 1982), 187.
2. Fee and Stuart, 189–190.
3. Francis I. Andersen, *Job: An Introduction and Commentary* (Downers Grove, IL: InterVarsity, 1984), 28.
4. Andersen, 36, 45.
5. This outline is adapted from Andersen, 75–76.

JOB 1:1–2:13

The Testing of Job

Shall we accept good from God, and not trouble?
(Job 2:10)

"In the land of Uz there lived a man . . ." This could
be the beginning of your story, or anyone's. Like
Job, we live on the stage of the world never knowing what is happening behind the scenes, on the
stage of heaven. Job never finds out what occurred
at the council of heaven, but his story gives us a
rare glimpse. When events seem inexplicable, it can
be encouraging to know that the council is at work
behind the scenes of our lives also.

Before beginning the questions in this lesson,
read 1:1–2:13. Thank God for letting you overhear
His divine council, and ask Him to teach you about
Himself through this opportunity.

First test (1:1-22)

Uz (1:1). See the map on page 9. Uz was somewhere
in *the East* (see 1:3); that is, east of the Jordan
River from Israel, south of Aram, and north of
Midian. The East "was the edge of civilization,
surrounded by an atmosphere of romance. It
was wild in parts, and from it came brigands to
maraud and pillage more settled folk. . . . In its
turn it was exposed to raids from bandits even
further out, such as the Sabeans and Chaldeans
(see Job 1:15,17). It was not desert, for in fertile

For Further Study:
Compare Job 1:1 to
Acts 24:16. Do you
fear God and shun
evil? How do your
actions show it? How
could you improve in
this area?

places there could be tillage and towns, at least
in good times. Here could be seen both nomadic
shepherd and settled farmer, and sometimes the
same person could be both."[1]

The exact location of Uz is unknown. It
may have been northeast of Galilee or possibly
in Edom.[2]

Blameless and upright (1:1). Not perfectly sinless,
but committed to integrity before God and man.
More specifically, Job was devout toward God
(**he feared God**) and moral toward people (**and
shunned evil**).

Seven . . . three (1:2). These numbers symbolized
completeness and were considered the ideal
numbers of sons and daughters.

He would sacrifice (1:5). Before God gave the Law
to Moses, the father of each household acted
as its priest (see Genesis 15:9-10). Job sent a
servant to his children to have them ritually
cleansed (**purified** or sanctified). Then he sacrificed animals to take away his children's sins.

Along with the fact that Job's wealth was in
livestock rather than land, his office as family
priest suggests that he lived before Moses. In
keeping with this historical setting, neither the
Law nor the temple nor any datable event is
mentioned in the book of Job.

Angels (1:6). Literally, "the sons of God." In a pas-
sionately monotheistic culture such as Israel,
no one would have imagined that the superhu-
man creatures who inhabited the heavens were
deities at all like God. The Lord of hosts reigned
supreme, for He had created all the rest. When
the angels assembled in the King's court, they
were there more to honor Him, listen to Him,
and take orders than to give Him counsel.

Satan (1:6). The Hebrew says "the Satan," which
means "the accuser." He has access to the
divine assembly, but God asks his business
there (see 1:7) because he is not a member of
the council.

My servant (1:8). The Lord consistently calls Job
this. The word means "slave," but in ancient

royal terminology it is an honor to be called the king's servant. It implies a special role in the administration. In the Old Testament, only a favored few such as Moses, David, and the prophets are called God's servants (see Exodus 14:31; 2 Samuel 3:18; Isaiah 41:8-9; Jeremiah 7:25).[3]

Fire of God (1:16). Usually lightning, or possibly volcanic fallout (see Genesis 19:24; 1 Kings 18:38). Only something strange could have wiped out seven thousand sheep.[4]

Tore his robe and shaved his head (1:20). Traditional acts of mourning. Job did not gash his skin, as pagans often did in mourning.[5]

For Thought and Discussion: What does it mean to fear God? In light of 1 John 4:18, is the fear of God inconsistent with the love of God? Why or why not? Are there different ways to fear God? Why or why not?

1. Job had rare qualities that delighted God (see 1:1,5,8). According to Satan, why did Job fear God (see 1:2-3,9-10)?

_____

_____

_____

_____

2. How did Satan's accusation disparage both God and Job?

God _____

_____

_____

_____

_____

Job _____

_____

_____

_____

_____

For Thought and Discussion: Why do you think God pointed out Job to Satan (see 1:8)? What was He trying to achieve?

For Thought and Discussion: Who or what was the cause of Job's sufferings? Was it God, Satan, Job, other people, random chance, or more than one of these?

3. In light of this, why do you think God gave Satan permission to afflict Job?

_____

_____

_____

_____

_____

4. In his first test (see 1:13-19), Job lost his wealth and his children. How did he respond to these losses, especially to the last one (see 1:20-22)?

_____

_____

_____

_____

5. Describe in your own words the attitudes (toward self, God, circumstances) you think Job was showing in 1:20-22.

_____

_____

_____

_____

_____

_____

_____

_____

Second test (2:1-10)

Skin for skin (2:4). A proverb with uncertain meaning. It may mean that a man will risk a lesser part of his body to protect a greater, or his outer skin to protect his inner one. Thus far, Satan has scratched only the outer surface of Job's life: his possessions and family. Satan implies that a man will gladly lose that outer skin if his own flesh is intact.[6]

Sat among the ashes (2:8). Probably in the refuse dump outside of town. Job scratched his itching sores with a shard of pottery.

Foolish (2:10). In the vocabulary of wisdom, this word means "lacking in moral discernment" rather than either "lacking in knowledge or intellect" or "wicked."[7]

Accept (2:10). "Receive" in RSV. The word implies active "co-operation with Providence, not mere submission."[8]

Trouble (2:10). "Evil" in RSV and KJV. The Hebrew word means anything bad and does not suggest that God is evil for sending it.[9] (See Isaiah 45:7; Amos 3:6.)

---

6. In the Lord's eyes, Job passed his first test with flying colors. However, what did cynical Satan think of Job's response to affliction (see 2:4-5)? (Explain in your own words.)

_____

_____

_____

_____

_____

7. Why did Job refuse to accuse God of wrong-doing, even though he knew his sufferings were not deserved punishment for sin (see 2:10)?

_____

_____

_____

For Thought and Discussion: Why didn't God just throw Satan out of the divine assembly and ignore his accusations? What do you learn about God from the way He takes Satan's charges seriously?

For Thought and Discussion: What was good about each of Job's reactions to his afflictions (see 1:20-22; 2:9-10)?

For Thought and Discussion: a. Does 1:1–2:10 suggest that Satan is God's equal? Why or why not?

b. Does the passage suggest that God is unable to prevent human suffering? Why or why not?

c. Does it suggest that God is less than perfectly good? Why or why not?

Optional Application: How can you apply Job's response to suffering to the way you deal with your own circumstances?

_____

_____

8. It is essential to the rest of the story that we, the readers, know the purpose of Job's suffering while Job and his friends do not. What is God's reason for allowing Job's anguish (see 1:9-11)?

_____

_____

_____

_____

_____

9. What can we learn from Job 1:1–2:10 about . . .

God (His character, abilities, nature, desires, methods)?

_____

_____

_____

_____

_____

_____

some possible reasons for human suffering?

_____

_____

_____

_____

_____

how a person should respond to suffering?

_____

_____

_____

_____

_____

_____

_____

_____

Job's friends (2:11-13)

Friends (2:11). The three men who visit Job in his
affliction seem from the dialogue to be elderly
sages, counselors in the wisdom tradition. They
come from different countries, so Job's fame as
a wise and righteous man must have won him
friends far and wide. ***Eliphaz the Temanite***
comes probably from Edom (see Genesis
36:11,15; Jeremiah 49:7,20). ***Bildad the Shuhite***
may come from Shuah, the middle region of
the Euphrates valley. The home of ***Zophar the
Naamathite*** is unknown.[10]

10. How did Job's three friends deal with his
calamity (see 2:11-13)?

_____

_____

_____

_____

_____

_____

_____

**Optional
Application:** Have
you ever experienced
severe economic
loss, bereavement of
loved ones, or painful
illness? How did you
feel about yourself,
life, God? How did
you act? Compare
yourself to Job. Would
you have passed Job's
test of not cursing
God? Why or why not?

**For Thought and
Discussion:** Is sitting
silently with a sufferer
a good or poor way to
sympathize with and
comfort him? Why?

Optional Application: Do you know anyone who is ill or bereaved? How can you best comfort that person?

Your response

Study Skill — Application

Second Timothy 3:16-17 says, "All Scripture . . . is useful for teaching, rebuking, correcting and training in righteousness, so that the servant of God may be thoroughly equipped for every good work." Paul also writes, "Everything that was written in the past was written to teach us, so that through the endurance taught in the Scriptures and the encouragement they provide we might have hope." (Romans 15:4), and "These things happened to them as examples and were written down as warnings for us" (1 Corinthians 10:11). Therefore, when you study Job, you should keep asking yourself, *What difference should this passage make in my life? How should it make me want to think or act? How does it encourage, warn, correct, or set me an example?*

Application will require time, thought, prayer, and perhaps even discussion with another person. You will usually find it more productive to concentrate on one specific application, giving it careful thought and prayer, than to list several potential applications without really reflecting on them or committing yourself to them. At other times, you may want to list many implications that a passage has for your life. Then you can choose one or two of these to act or meditate upon.

Question 9 allows you to summarize your insights on the three central issues of 1:1–2:10, and question 10 points to the essence of 2:11-13. You can look to these and the optional questions for ideas on application.

---

11. Review your answers to questions 1 through 10. What one insight from 1:1–2:13 would you like to apply to your own life?

_____

_____

_____

_____

_____

_____

Optional Application: How should knowing what went on in heaven in Job's case affect your response to circumstances?

12. How would you like this truth to affect you? (How do you fall short? How does the insight apply to you?)

_____

_____

_____

_____

_____

13. Think of at least one specific action you can take to grow in this area. It can be prayer, meditation, talking to someone, making a choice and sticking to it, and so on.

_____

_____

_____

_____

14. If you have any questions about 1:1–2:13, record them here. You can ask the members of your group, research them in one of the resources listed on pages 123–125, or ask another Christian you trust.

_____

_____

_____

_____

For the group

Warm-up. The experiences of each group member are going to affect how he or she interprets and applies the book of Job. You will understand each other's views much better if you know some of those experiences. Over the next few weeks, you might begin each meeting by letting one person briefly share one of his or her experiences of affliction or bereavement: What happened? How did you feel? What did you do? The group shouldn't discuss what the person *should* have done, since people are sensitive to criticism in painful areas like these. Just try to understand each other and identify with Job and one another. Don't force anyone to share more deeply than he or she feels comfortable with; it may take you some time to develop trust, and some people may still be hurting.

Read aloud. It is usually a good idea to read a passage silently or aloud just before discussing it. This refreshes everyone's memory and puts you into the mood of the passage. In later lessons that deal with many passages, we'll suggest one or two short ones to read aloud. However, 1:1–2:13 should not be too much to read. To make this more fun, you might assign the parts of narrator, God, Satan, and Job to different people.

Summarize. To begin your discussion, ask someone to tell in a sentence or two what happens in 1:1–2:13. What is the story about? It is a good idea to step back and glance at the forest before examining each tree.

Job's tests. The two focuses of this lesson are: (1) God—His character, His ways, and His reasons for doing what He does, and (2) how Job responded to both prosperity and suffering, and how we should respond. Both understanding God and knowing how to live are important. But you may not be able to fully discuss both, so you should decide which will interest your group most and choose your discussion questions accordingly. Questions 2, 3, 8, and 9, the first "For Thought and Discussion" on page 22, and the first on page 23 deal with God's ways. The two latter questions are as important as the numbered ones, but they are not easy, fill-in-the-blank questions. They will make good discussion questions.

Notice what Satan isn't: He isn't a rival king equal to God, and he isn't able to do anything without God's permission. But don't spend a lot of time on Satan. He is a minor character in this book; God and Job are the focuses.

You may sometimes want to flesh out the study with observation and interpretation questions. For instance, question 1 assumes an observation ("What were Job's qualities that please God?") and several interpretations ("What does it mean to be blameless and upright? To fear God? To shun evil?") Sometimes the study guide explains words such as these, while at other times you will have to think for yourselves.

You might not be able to cover every question in a lesson with equal depth. There is nothing wrong with skipping some questions, adding some optional questions, or spending all your time on two or three questions.

As a rule, it is good to plan half your time to discuss how the passage applies to you. Encourage everyone to think of at least one specific way to apply some insight, but don't insist that each person have a new application every week. People will sometimes want to think about the same discovery for several weeks before taking any concrete action or moving to another application. If someone can't find anything in a passage that demands immediate action, urge him or her to choose something to meditate or pray about. Some people may not yet feel comfortable telling their specific applications to the group; if so, you might look for ways to build trust and intimacy over the next few weeks.

Summarize. Ask a few people to summarize your discussion. Question 9 will have done this in part, but this is your chance to clarify what you want to remember from 1:1–2:13. Summarize areas of disagreement as well as those of consensus if you found yourselves disagreeing. You can also summarize how you plan to apply the passage.

Worship. Praise God for what you learned about Him in 1:1–2:13. Praise Him for the way He deals with Satan's accusations. Meditate together on the attitudes Job shows in 1:20-22 and 2:10. Ask God to give you those attitudes and to be with you in the midst of the afflictions you are experiencing. Pray specifically for the needs of group members.

The Names of God

On a casual reading of Job in English, one might not notice how many names for God are used in the book, nor grasp their significance. Among these names are:

1. **El, Eloah.** These are both translated "God" in English versions. *El* was the Hebrew word for God or god in general, and *Eloah* is a variant of it. In Canaanite religion, *El* was the father and king of all the gods who seldom bothered with human affairs. *El* and *Eloah* are used often and interchangeably in the dialogues.

2. **Elohim.** This is also translated "God" in English. *Elohim* is plural, and when used with plural verbs it means "gods." When used with singular verbs, as in Job, it is the "plural of majesty," meaning something like "God of gods." (In a similar way, the ferocious creature of 40:15-24 is called *Behemoth*, which means literally "beasts" and implies "beast of beasts.") *Elohim* is the only word for "God" in the prologue (see Job chapters 1 and 2). It is also used occasionally in the speeches, but less than *El* and *Eloah*. In 20:29, Zophar speaks of *Elohim* in the first half of the verse and *El* in the second half.

3. **Shaddai.** This is translated "the Almighty" in English. *Shaddai* probably means "the Mountain One," a reference to God's mountainous power.

4. **YHWH.** Most English versions render this as "the Lord," while a few guess at its pronunciation as "Yahweh" or "Jehovah." *YHWH* is the personal name of Israel's God. It is related to the Hebrew for "I Am" (Exodus 3:14) — not just "I exist" but "I am actively present." *YHWH* is actively present with His people in the midst of their needs. He revealed the meaning of this name to Israel when the people were slaves in Egypt and *YHWH* rescued them.

Because Hebrew was not written with vowels and because the Jews came to regard God's name as too holy to be spoken, we don't know how it should be pronounced. The Jews say

Adonai ("my Lord") when reading Scripture or talking about *YHWH*. This is why "the Lᴏʀᴅ" is a common English rendering. "Jehovah" is a combination of the constants of *YHWH* with the vowels of *Adonai*. "Yahweh" is the best guess of modern scholars.

In Job, *YHWH* occurs often in the narrative sections: the prologue, introductions in God's speeches, and the epilogue. It occurs only once in chapters 3–37, in 12:9. This unique use of the Divine Name suggests to some scholars that 12:9 is a key verse for understanding the book.

5. **Adonai.** In Job, this occurs only in 28:28. Proverbs 1:7, 9:10, and similar passages speak of "the fear of *YHWH*," but Job 28:28 has "the fear of *Adonai*." This word emphasizes His lordship over all creation.

6. **Qadosh.** This is "the Holy One" in 6:10. Isaiah likes to speak of "the Holy One of Israel," but it is rare and probably meant for special impact elsewhere in the Old Testament. Job emphasizes that he has not committed the heinous sin of denying the holy words of the Holy One.[11]

1. Francis I. Andersen, *Job: An Introduction and Commentary* (Downers Grove, IL: InterVarsity, 1984), 77.
2. Andersen, 77; Marvin H. Pope, *Job: Introduction, Translation, and Notes* (Garden City, NY: Doubleday, 1973), 3–4.
3. Andersen, 84; Kenneth Barker, ed., *The NIV Study Bible* (Grand Rapids, MI: Zondervan, 1985), 735, 1074, 1076.
4. Andersen, 87.
5. Andersen, 87.
6. Andersen, 90; Pope, 20.
7. Andersen, 93.
8. Andersen, 93.
9. Andersen, 93.
10. Andersen, 94–95; Pope, 23–24; Barker, 737.
11. J. A. Motyer, "The Names of God," *Eerdmans' Handbook to the Bible*, ed. David and Pat Alexander (Grand Rapids, MI: Eerdmans, 1973), 157; Robert Young, *Young's Analytical Concordance to the Bible* (Grand Rapids, MI: Eerdmans, 1970), 28, 411–418, 488, 617–618.

JOB 3:1–27:23

Job in Anguish

Oh, for the days when I was in my prime,
when God's intimate friendship blessed my house.
(Job 29:4)

In 1:20-22 and 2:10, Job reacted impressively to his afflictions. God was right: Job did not lose his fear of God when immediate rewards were removed. But as day passes into day, and Job's sores still ooze, and his bereavement and desolation weigh on his mind, Job begins to waver. At last he breaks the silence he has shared with his friends and expresses his feelings about his life and the God who has created it.

Have you ever lost health or loved ones, or have you ever known someone who has? As you study the following passages, try to put yourself in Job's and his friends' places and truly empathize with not only their feelings but also their understanding of God.

Study Skill — Paraphrasing
A good way to be sure you understand a passage is to restate it in your own words. In this study, when you are asked to tell what someone says in some passage, summarize the poetry in your own words. (You can include words from the passage also if you are sure you understand them.) If you aren't sure about the meaning, compare several Bible versions.

For Thought and Discussion: a. Have you ever wished you had never been born or that you could die soon? If so, why?

b. What would have helped or did help you let go of this desire?

c. What can you do to help others — Christian or non-Christian — let go of the desire not to be alive?

1. Satan predicted that Job would curse God (see 2:5). Does Job do this in chapter 3? Explain.

_____

_____

_____

_____

_____

2. Why does Job long for death?

3:11-15 _____

3:23 _____

_____

7:1-5 _____

_____

3. What are the things that give Job anguish?

7:1-6 _____

_____

_____

9:1-20 _____

_____

_____

9:27-31 _____

_____

12:4 _____

19:7 _____

_____

_____

19:8-20 _____

_____

_____

_____

29:1-6 _____

_____

29:7-25 _____

_____

30:1-23 _____

_____

_____

30:25-26 _____

_____

For Thought and Discussion: Has Job abandoned what he said in 1:20-22 and 2:10? Why or why not?

4. From chapters 29–30, what has happened to Job's relationships . . .

with people? _____

_____

_____

with God? _____

_____

_____

_____

5. How does Job describe his feelings?

6:2-3 _____

_____

6:14 _____

7:11 _____

10:1 _____

_____

30:27 _____

6. In your judgment, are Job's feelings understandable, correct, and/or justifiable? Which ones are, and which aren't? Why?

_____

_____

_____

_____

_____

7. How do you think you would feel in Job's place?

_____

_____

_____

_____

_____

8. To what extent can you identify with Job right now, and why?

_____

_____

_____

_____

_____

9. Put yourself in Job's friends' place. You don't know about the agreement between God and Satan; you know only that Job has suffered terrible losses of his wealth, children, and health. What would you say to him or do after hearing his cries?

_____

_____

_____

_____

_____

_____

_____

_____

For Thought and Discussion: What do you think of Job's honesty about his feelings? Are you able to be that honest with God? With other Christians?

Your response

Study Skill — Application

Job is not always a good example for us to follow. Not everything he says is true. Yet in 42:7, God affirms that Job's words about God have been basically right. Also, as an outspoken human being, Job can help us understand the deep feelings we and others may not feel comfortable expressing. Some questions to ask yourself when trying to apply the book of Job are:

1. Is what this person says true? What does the rest of Scripture say about this? Does my own experience coincide with this?

2. Have I ever felt this way? Do I feel this way now? Does anyone I know feel this way? How should I respond?

---

10. What have you learned from this lesson that is significant or relevant to your life?

_____

_____

_____

_____

11. Is there any action you would like to take to apply what you have learned? If so, describe it.

_____

_____

_____

_____

_____

_____

12. List any questions you have about this lesson.

_____

_____

_____

_____

For the group

Warm-up. Let one or two people describe an experience of suffering they have had and how they responded to it.

Read aloud. To set the tone of Job's feelings, have someone read chapter 3 aloud. Ask him or her to use the tone of voice Job might have used in speaking these words.

Summarize. This lesson focuses on how Job feels and why. Before beginning on the questions, ask someone to summarize in a sentence or two how Job feels.

Questions. Questions 1 through 5 lay the groundwork for your evaluations and personal sharing in questions 6 through 8. Take time to understand Job's feelings, and then share what you think of them. Because Job is a deeply intimate book, you will need to make a special effort to establish trust among group members. Agree together that nothing shared in the group will be repeated elsewhere. If you find your group reluctant to become personal, ask members why either in the meeting or in private.

Prayer. Thank God for the birth of each person in the room. If any of you finds it difficult to be glad you were born, ask the group to pray for you. Pray also for anyone else who is feeling anguish.

Hebrew Poetry

English poetry (except free verse) is based on lines of even length and rhythm that often rhyme. Hebrew poetry is not. As an example, compare Psalm 23:1-2 in your Bible to this rendition in the Scottish Psalter:

> The Lord's my shepherd, I'll not want.
> He makes me down to lie
> In pastures green: he leadeth me
> The quiet waters by.

Hebrew poetry is based on parallelism of ideas. Successive lines intensify an idea by repetition or contrast, sometimes in intricate patterns. For instance, look at Job 27:4. The basic unit is a *line* or *colon*. A period is a unit of one or more colons that is a complete thought. Job 27:4 is a period made of two colons, a *bicolon*:

> My lips will not say anything wicked,
>   and my tongue will not utter lies.

The colons are parallel because each element of the second colon matches one in the first:

my lips	my tongue
will not speak	will not utter
wickedness	deceit

In a *tricolon* (a period with three lines, such as Job 30:15), even more patterns are possible. It is also common to have the second line or a bicolon contrast the first, as in Hosea 7:14. Or the second line can build on the first in some other way. Periods for one, four, and even five colons are used for special effect (such as Job 28:22 or 38:2). Job 14:1 has the parallelism within each line.

A group of periods is called a *strophe* (pronounced "stro-fee"). The group can be arranged in a variety of patterns, so when we read a passage of Job, we might find ideas organized in what seem like strange orders. For example, we expect

(continued on page 40)

(continued from page 39)

to find the main or high point at the beginning or end and the details grouped logically. However, in Job the point is often in the middle, and contrasting ideas may come before and after. A group of strophes may be called a *passage* or *poem,* so the organization can be quite intricate.

For instance, in 13:28–14:12 and 14:18-22, Job discusses the brevity of human life. In between, he declares his hope for resurrection. Again, in 19:1-22, Job accuses his friends and God of tormenting him. There is a climax of faith in 19:23-27, and then Job returns to the former mood in 19:28-29. As 13:15 falls in the middle of a poem, so you will often find the high points of faith in the midst of doubts and accusations.

When you study a passage of Job, don't worry about seeing the patterns perfectly. Just be aware that the order may seem jumbled at first glance, and try to get the gist of the whole.[1]

1. Francis I. Andersen, *Job: An Introduction and Commentary* (Downers Grove, IL: InterVarsity, 1984), 37–41.

Lesson Four

JOB 3:1–27:23

The Friends Respond

Those who are at ease have contempt
for misfortune as the fate of those
whose feet are slipping.
(Job 12:5)

You've heard Job's anguish—he doesn't hide his
feelings. You've had a chance to consider what
you would say or do if you were Job's friend. Keep
question 9 of lesson 3 in mind as you examine how
Job's three visitors do respond to his vent of emotions.

1. The visitors speak in turn throughout the book,
   but their counsel to Job is fairly consistent.
   They diagnose the reason for his suffering and
   advise what Job should do. What is each man's
   diagnosis?

   Eliphaz (see 4:7-8; 5:17; 22:4-11) _____

   _____

   _____

   _____

   _____

   _____

   Bildad (see 8:3-4,8-20) _____

   _____

41

_____

_____

_____

Zophar (see 11:11-12) _____

_____

_____

_____

2. Job's friends base their counsel on the traditional teaching of wisdom, which defines how God deals with people according to justice. According to this classical statement of justice, what does God do to the wicked and the righteous? (See Deuteronomy 28:1-2,15; Psalm 37:17; Galatians 6:7-8.)

wicked _____

_____

_____

_____

_____

righteous _____

_____

_____

_____

_____

3. In light of the cross-references in question 2, are Job's friends generally correct or incorrect in their theory about the way God acts? Why?

_____

_____

_____

4. Are they correct in applying this system to Job's situation? What has God said about this that the friends don't know (see 2:3-6)?

_____

_____

_____

_____

_____

_____

5. The book of Romans makes it clear that every human being has a sinful nature and commits sins and that every human being therefore deserves God's wrath. (See, for example, Romans 3:9-10,23; 5:12; 6:23.) Does this help us understand Job's situation?

   a. Does Job deny that he is a sinner? What does he say about this in these passages?

   7:21 _____

   _____

   9:2 _____

   _____

   14:13-17 _____

   _____

   _____

   _____

   23:11-12 _____

   _____

   _____

   _____

   _____

For Thought and Discussion: On page 20, we saw that "blameless" (1:1,8; 2:3) does not mean "sinless" but rather "committed to integrity." Job sacrificed sin offerings for his children (see 1:5), and we have no reason to doubt that he confessed and sacrificed for his own sins also. What, then, might Job mean when he says, "I am blameless" (9:21) and "I am not guilty" (10:7)?

b. Are Job's friends saying that his sufferings are deserved because of his sinful nature or because of some specific, especially wicked sin that he is hiding? (Recall your answer to question 1.)

_____

_____

_____

_____

c. From what you know from the prologue, is Job suffering because he is a sinner like all men? Explain.

_____

_____

_____

_____

_____

d. How valid is it, then, to explain an individual's sufferings by pointing out that all people are sinners and deserve wrath?

_____

_____

_____

_____

6. Like any God-fearing man of his day, Job believes in the system you described in question 2. Knowing his own conscience (see question 5a), what conclusions might Job be tempted to draw about God? (See, for instance, 19:6.)

_____

_____

_____
_____
_____

7. How do Job's friends feel about his questions and doubts of God (see 8:1-3; 11:1-6)?

_____
_____
_____
_____

8. What is wrong with the counsel of Job's friends? What do the following passages reveal?

1:1-5 _____
_____
_____

6:14-21 _____
_____
_____
_____

12:3 _____
_____
_____

12:4-5; 16:4-5 _____
_____
_____
_____

For Thought and Discussion: Are Zophar and Elihu right or wrong in 11:4 and 33:8-9? Why is this a crucial issue?

Optional Application: How is the difference between being sinless and being blameless and upright personally important to you?

9. Summarize what you have observed in this lesson about . . .

the issues Job struggled with as he strove to maintain faith in God in the midst of suffering

_____

_____

_____

_____

_____

how not to counsel someone in pain _____

_____

_____

_____

_____

_____

Your response

> **Study Skill — Application**
> It can be helpful to plan an application in five steps:
>   1. Record the verse or passage that contains the truth you want to apply to your life. If the passage is short enough, consider copying it word for word as an aid to memory. If it is too long, just record the reference (for instance, 6:14).
>   2. State the truth of the passage that impresses you. For example, "Pat answers to someone's suffering aren't Christlike, even if they are generally true scriptural principles. A person in despair should receive devotion and compassion, even if his faith seems to be wavering and he is saying scandalous things

about God. Principles can be discussed when grief and pain have been assuaged."

3. Tell how you fall short in relation to this truth. (Ask God to enable you to see yourself clearly.) For instance, "When someone is hurting, I tend to quote Scripture to him instead of listening. I'm so concerned with keeping the person from falling into error or indulging in complaining that I seem harsh and uncaring. Because of this, I often don't meet the real need. I need to spend more time listening and less time talking, even when the person is wrong."

4. State precisely what you plan to do about having your life changed in this area. (Ask God what, if anything, you can do. Don't forget that transformation depends on His will, power, and timing, not on yours. Diligent prayer should always be part of your application.) For example, "I don't know anyone right now who is needing someone to listen, but I'm going to ask God to lead me to someone who is. I will also memorize Job 6:14 and pray daily this week that God will make me a devoted friend, not a critic. I wonder if anyone in my family is in need of a devoted friend."

5. Plan a way to remind yourself to do what you have decided, such as putting a note on your refrigerator or in your office or asking a friend or relative to remind you.[1]

10. What insights from this lesson seem relevant to your life?

_____

_____

_____

_____

_____

_____

_____

_____

For Thought and Discussion: To what extent do you feel that your own sufferings are due to your own sins?

11. How would you like what you have learned to affect your attitudes and behaviors?

_____

_____

_____

_____

_____

12. Is there anything you would like to do or pray about what you've learned to help this transformation take place? If so, write down your plans.

_____

_____

_____

_____

13. List any questions you have about this lesson.

_____

_____

_____

_____

For the group

Warm-up. Let everyone think about the following question for a minute or two: "To what extent do you feel that your own sufferings are due to your own sins?" You can come back to this question later, if you like, but at this point it is just to get everyone thinking personally.

Read aloud. To remember the sense of Job's friends' words, have someone read chapter 8 of Job aloud with the tone of voice he or she thinks Bildad might have used.

Summarize. This lesson lays out a central theme of the book: the friends' interpretation of Job's sufferings and how it relates both to the traditional wisdom doctrine and to the real facts from the prologue.

Questions. The questions lead you systematically to some conclusions. Question 5 goes into great detail to make sure everyone understands what the book of Job isn't about. Neither Job nor his friends deny that all people are sinners and deserve wrath. But the friends interpret Scripture to be saying that suffering is always a punishment proportional to the degree of sin. After all, the three friends are also sinners, but they are doing fine. And Job was doing great also until his sudden reversal. The friends conclude that Job must have committed some specific, serious, willful sin that he is hiding. The only other possibility seems to be that God is being whimsical and not following the laws of justice. Of course God has a right to afflict any sinner, but the issue is "Why Job?" From the prologue, we know that God isn't claiming to be fair according to the friends' standards; He is operating by a higher justice to achieve a greater good than the men suspect.

These are not easy concepts. If the details elude some members of your group, try anyway to arrive at some principles for understanding suffering and helping those who are suffering. Encourage everyone to come up with an application, even if it is only a truth to meditate on.

Worship. Praise God for His justice—for the rules stated in Scripture and for His decisions that are higher than our comprehension. Praise Him for giving you glimpses into the mysteries of suffering and justice.

1. This "Five-Point Application" is based on the method in *Course 4*, THE 2:7 SERIES (Colorado Springs, CO: NavPress, 1979), 50–51.

JOB 3:1-37:24

God the Enemy

I cry out to you, God, but you do not answer;
I stand up, but you merely look at me.
(Job 30:20)

Job and his friends agree that justice would require
God to afflict the wicked and prosper the righteous.
But based on this belief, the men have come to
opposite interpretations of Job's situation. The three
sages have concluded that Job must have earned his
suffering by some awful hidden sin; if he will only
repent, he will be healed. Job knows that although
he is a sinner, he is innocent of known, unrepented
sin, so he is forced to begin to question God's justice
and goodness. This is no academic matter; the most
important thing in Job's life—his faith in and relationship with God—is at stake.

   Have you ever found your situation incompatible with what you believe about God? Try to
remember or imagine what that feels like.

1. Having concluded that Job is being punished for
   some sin, what do his friends advise him to do?

   Eliphaz (see 4:6; 5:8,17-19; 22:22-26) _____

   _____

   _____

   _____

**For Thought and
Discussion:** Would
the friends' advice
(question 1) generally
be good or poor
action for a person to
take? Why?

For Further Study:
Compare Job's words
in questions 2 and 3
to the thoughts and
feelings expressed
in Psalm 42. How
common do you think
these feelings are?

_____

_____

Bildad (see 8:5-7) _____

_____

_____

_____

Zophar (see 11:13-17) _____

_____

_____

_____

2. Job finds this advice cruel (see 6:15). Why?

6:25,28-30 _____

_____

_____

7:20-21 _____

_____

_____

9:2-3 _____

_____

_____

13:20-24 _____

_____

_____

23:3-9 _____

_____

_____

_____

30:20 _____

_____

_____

For Thought and Discussion: Think about 30:20. Have you ever felt that God was silent, refusing to answer your agonized cries? How did you feel about Him and yourself? Looking back, can you see any reasons for His silence? How do you feel about that situation now?

3. Why does God's apparent silence grieve Job so severely (see 1:1; 29:1-6)?

_____

_____

_____

_____

4. Unlike Job, we know why God won't explain His reasons for allowing Job to suffer. Why is God silent (see 1:6-12; 2:1-6)?

_____

_____

_____

_____

_____

5. Since God won't explain why He has afflicted Job, and since Job can recall no unconfessed sin that merits awful punishment beyond what other men receive, Job begins to wonder about God. What does Job say and ask about God's actions in these passages?

10:2-7 _____

_____

_____

_____

_____

Optional Application: Have you ever felt that God was treating you as an enemy? Explain. How do you view that situation now? Do you think you were correct about God's malice toward you? Why or why not? Talk with God about your feelings.

10:13-17 _____

_____

_____

_____

_____

16:7-17 _____

_____

_____

_____

_____

19:6-22 _____

_____

_____

_____

_____

6. What do Job's words imply about God's character?

_____

_____

_____

_____

7. Job knows that his questions and complaints are rash (see 6:3) and that he is behaving impatiently (see 6:11; 21:4). Why does he think his impatience is understandable, if not positively justified (see 6:1-3,11-13)?

_____

_____

_____

_____

_____

For Further Study:
a. Read Romans 11:33-
36. Is this relevant
to your answers in
questions 8 and 9?
Why or why not?
  b. Would it be
appropriate or helpful
to quote this passage
to a person in Job's
situation? Why or why
not?

8. Think about what Job is going through and the fact that he doesn't know why. (If necessary, review 1:18-19, 2:7-8, and 7:5, or read 30:1-15.) To what extent are Job's words in question 5 *accurate*, given what we know from the prologue (see 1:6-12; 2:1-6)?

_____

_____

_____

_____

_____

_____

9. Now, to what extent are Job's statements in question 5 *reasonable*, given what Job does and doesn't know? To what extent are they ungodly even for a man in his situation? Give reasons for your opinions.

_____

_____

_____

_____

_____

_____

10. What dangers do Job's friends find in statements like those in question 5?

8:3 _____

_____

15:4 _____

_____

For Thought and Discussion: a. Does question 5 suggest that Job has lost faith in God? Are his doubts and questions incompatible with faith? Why or why not?

b. Reconsider this question after studying more of Job's words in later lessons. Or look now at 42:7-8. Has Job "spoken of me [God] what is right" in the passages in question 5? How, or why not?

11. In your judgment, are the friends correct? Why or why not?

_____

_____

_____

_____

_____

_____

12. The young man Elihu has an explanation for God's silence when men pray: God ignores prayers from those who are wicked or whose love for and faith in God are imperfect (see Job 35:9-16). How true and helpful is Elihu's explanation (see Job 2:3-10; James 4:3; 1 John 3:21-24)?

_____

_____

_____

_____

_____

13. How do you think Job should have responded to God's silence? (Support your answer with Scripture and careful thought. Try to avoid being either unbiblical or unfeeling. Consider some of the cross-references in the margin of page 57.)

_____

_____

_____

_____

_____

_____

Your response

14. What would you say to Job if he said in front of you what he said in question 5? (Would you say what you wrote in question 13 or something else? Why?)

_____

_____

_____

_____

_____

15. Is anything in this lesson relevant to your life? If so, what insight would you like to take to heart?

_____

_____

_____

_____

16. How would you like this insight to affect your life?

_____

_____

_____

_____

_____

17. What, if anything, do you plan to do about what you have learned? (Consider prayer and action.)

_____

_____

For Thought and Discussion: a. Do you think someone should remind Job of Philippians 4:4-9,12-13? Why or why not?

b. Do you think Job should try to rejoice in the Lord and be quietly content with his circumstances? Why or why not?

c. In your judgment, do Psalm 22:1-21, 2 Corinthians 1:8-11, or James 5:13-16 suggest ways Job should have responded to his circumstances? Why or why not?

For Thought and Discussion: Compare your answers to questions 13 and 14 to the ways Job's friends handle the situation. How is your approach similar and different?

_____

_____

_____

18. List any questions you have about this lesson.

_____

_____

_____

_____

For the group

Warm-up. Ask one or two people to tell about a time when they felt that God was silent. What were the circumstances? How did you feel? What did you do?

Questions. If the group is having trouble understanding some of the passages, consider consulting a commentary (see page 123 for some suggestions). Also, examine just a few passages for each question, comparing several translations and asking the group what the passages mean.

Some questions in this and other lessons (such as 9, 11, 12, and 13) ask you to evaluate what Job and his friends say. Help group members base their opinions on the rest of Scripture and on what the prologue of Job tells you. If you don't know enough Scripture to be confident about your opinions, examine them to see what they are based on. Your group should be open to hearing everyone's opinions without ridicule but should also sift opinions to discern flaws.

In order to allow time for personal application, you may want to discuss only a few of the questions.

Worship. Praise God for what you know about Him, despite what circumstances and emotions sometimes imply. Tell Him honestly any feelings, doubts, or suspicions you have about Him. Ask Him to help you see Him as He is.

Lesson Six

JOB 3:1–37:24

The Sovereign Lord

He stands alone, and who can oppose him?
He does whatever he pleases.
(Job 23:13)

Job and his friends agree on one thing about God:
He is Boss of the universe. However, they find
drastically different implications in this fact. As
you study the passages in this lesson, ask the Lord
to reveal Himself to you and show you how His
majesty should affect your life.

1. Eliphaz speaks for all three friends in 5:9-16.
   What does he say God does?

   _____

   _____

   _____

   _____

   _____

   _____

   _____

2. In Eliphaz's opinion, how should these facts
   about God make Job *feel* and *act* (see 5:8,17-27)?

   feel _____

   _____

For Thought and Discussion: How accurate is Job's description of God in the passages in question 3? What, if anything, does he say that is untrue? What are the implications of this for you?

_____

_____

act _____

_____

_____

_____

3. Job acknowledges that God is all-powerful. In the following passages, what does Job say the Omnipotent One does with His power?

9:1-13 _____

_____

_____

_____

_____

_____

12:13-25 _____

_____

_____

_____

_____

_____

26:5-14 _____

_____

_____

_____

_____

4. How do these acts make God seem to you? (Comfortable? Easy to handle?) Compare your answer to question 2.

_____

_____

_____

_____

_____

5. What does Job think are the implications of such power?

9:14-20 _____

_____

_____

_____

_____

23:13-16 _____

_____

_____

_____

_____

6. How does God's power make Job feel (see 23:15)?

_____

_____

_____

_____

7. Do you think Job's feelings about God are good, understandable, and/or misguided? Why?

_____

_____

**Optional
Application:** Is Job's
attitude in 23:17 an
example for you
to follow or avoid
following in your
circumstances? Why?
Specifically how can
you put this into
practice?

8. a. Despite his feelings (see 23:15-16), how does
Job resolve to behave toward the all-powerful
God and the circumstances He has sent (see
23:17)?

_____

_____

_____

_____

b. What do you think of this attitude?

_____

_____

_____

_____

_____

9. When the young man Elihu finally speaks, what
does he say about God (see 36:5,22-33; 37:1-
24)? Write down any observations you want to
remember.

_____

_____

_____

_____

_____

_____

_____

_____

Your response

Optional Application: Choose some verses from this lesson to memorize and think about this week. Copy them on something to keep with you.

10. How do you think a person should speak about and treat the God whom Job and his friends have described? Give some specific examples that apply to you.

_____

_____

_____

_____

_____

_____

11. Does God's greatness move you to any response? How should His nature affect your prayers, attitudes, and plans for this week?

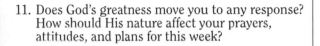

_____

_____

_____

12. Write down any questions you have about the passages in this lesson.

_____

_____

_____

_____

For the group

Warm-up. Ask each person to name one way in which he or she has experienced or observed God's power recently. When everyone has spoken, ask the group if mostly pleasant or mostly uncomfortable things were named. What does this tell you about your views of God?

Questions. After discussing questions 1 and 2, read aloud some of the passages in question 3. Then discuss questions 3 through 8. Next, read part of what Elihu says in question 9, and compare Job's and Elilhu's view of God. How true is each view? How should they move you to treat God? Look for specific answers to questions 10 and 11.

Worship. Praise God for all the ways He reveals His power to you. Use some of the passages in Job as springboards to worship.

Lesson Seven

JOB 3:1–37:24

The Judge

> *Your hands shaped me and made me.*
> *Will you now turn and destroy me?*
> *Remember that you molded me like clay.*
> *Will you now turn me to dust again?* . . .
> *Though I cry, "Violence!"*
> *I get no response;*
> *though I call for help, there is no justice.*
> *(Job 10:8-9; 19:7)*

Job doesn't doubt God's power for a minute. Job is sure that if the Lord wanted to do so He could vanquish the wicked and restore the faithful to health and happiness. But this is exactly what the Almighty is not doing in Job's life. Is God really as just and good as Job has always believed?

1. What does Job know about God, according to 10:8-12?

   _____

   _____

   _____

2. Therefore, what does Job find incomprehensible?

   10:8-9,13-17 _____

   _____

   _____

65

_____

_____

7:17-21 _____

_____

_____

_____

3:20-23 _____

_____

_____

_____

3. How do Job's friends defend God's justice (see 8:1-7,20; 11:5-6)?

_____

_____

_____

_____

_____

_____

4. How does Job respond to this defense?

9:22-24 _____

_____

_____

_____

12:6 _____

_____

_____

_____

12:16 _____

_____

_____

19:6-7 _____

_____

_____

21:4-21 _____

_____

_____

_____

_____

21:22-26 _____

_____

_____

_____

21:27-34 _____

_____

_____

_____

30:26 _____

_____

_____

_____

For Thought and Discussion: a. Read what Job accuses his friends of in 13:7-12. Why does Job think they have been showing wrong partiality to God? Consider their words in question 3.

b. From 42:7-8, does it seem that Job is right in 13:7-12? Does God abhor ignorant defense of His justice? Why or why not?

c. How should all this affect the way you deal with people who question God's actions?

5. Is Job correct in 9:22-24 and 21:4-34 that the wicked often prosper and the righteous suffer? Support your view with evidence from Scripture and your own experience.

_____

_____

For Thought and Discussion: Whose idea of God is bigger and more sovereign: Job's or his friends'? Why do you think so?

_____

_____

_____

_____

_____

6. What do the friends say to justify God?

11:7-10 _____

_____

_____

11:11-12 _____

_____

_____

22:1-11 _____

_____

_____

_____

_____

_____

34:10-20 _____

_____

_____

_____

_____

34:29 _____

_____

_____

35:1-8 _____

_____

_____

_____

_____

36:22-26 _____

_____

_____

_____

_____

7. Do the assertions of Job's visitors satisfy you? Why or why not?

_____

_____

_____

_____

8. Job can't see how it can be right that God lets an innocent man suffer. What doesn't he know about the reasons for innocent suffering?

Job 2:3-6 _____

_____

_____

_____

_____

John 9:1-3 _____

_____

_____

_____

_____

2 Corinthians 1:3-5 _____

_____

_____

_____

2 Corinthians 1:8-11 _____

_____

_____

2 Corinthians 4:7-12,16-18 _____

_____

_____

_____

Hebrews 2:10-11; 4:15 _____

_____

_____

_____

_____

A special case: Isaiah 53:1-12; Mark 15:12-39;
Hebrews 2:18

_____

_____

_____

_____

_____

Your response

For Further Study:
Job wasn't the only Old Testament believer who questioned why God didn't always follow the traditional teaching about the righteous prospering and the wicked suffering. See Psalm 73:1-28 and Jeremiah 12:1-6 for more questioners and their insights.

9. What would you say to a person who doubts God's goodness in the face of inexplicable affliction?

_____

_____

_____

_____

_____

_____

_____

10. Is anything in this lesson relevant to your life? If so, what is it, how is it relevant, and how might you respond to it?

_____

_____

_____

_____

_____

_____

_____

11. List any questions you have about the passages in this lesson.

_____

_____

_____

_____

For the group

Warm-up. Ask the group to think of examples of people suffering when they appear to have done nothing in particular to deserve it.

Questions. When a question has many passages, such as questions 4 and 6, you can ask each person to tell what one of the passages contributes to answering it. Strive for specific reasons and evidence for such questions as 5, 7, and 9. Tie your answers to particular passages and your own experiences.

Worship. Praise God for His inscrutable justice that defies our neat rules and formulas. Thank Him for giving you insight into the mystery of innocent suffering. If some of you still have doubts about the way God is treating you, pray for each other to have personal reassurance from the Lord.

Lesson Eight

JOB 3:1-37:24

Job Demands a Trial

> *I desire to speak to the Almighty*
> *and to argue my case with God. . . .*
> *Though he slay me, yet will I hope in him;*
> *I will surely defend my ways to his face.*
> *(Job 13:3,15)*

Because of God's silence in the face of Job's suffering, Job began to question God's goodness and justice. Job's friends have urged him to call upon the Almighty for pardon, but Job knows of nothing to confess. Still, calling upon the Lord has always been his habit, and he keeps it up.

The pledge you demand (17:3). A figure of speech used in the business world of Job's time. The pledge is a "material token of commitment to a commercial transaction," like the seal Judah gives in Genesis 38:18. **Security** in 17:3 is literally "striking hands," the gesture that signifies an agreement. Job wants God to provide the guarantees that He and Job are partners, not enemies—that Job's suffering is not punishment for sin.[1]

---

1. Not once in all the book does Job ask God to restore his possessions or heal his illness. However, what does he plead for over and over?

   10:1-2 _____

For Thought and Discussion: Job addresses God repeatedly and wants to confront Him. Job's friends only talk about Him. Is there any significance in this? If so, what?

_____

_____

13:3 _____

_____

_____

13:20-22 _____

_____

14:13-17 _____

_____

_____

_____

_____

17:3-4 _____

_____

_____

31:5-6 _____

_____

_____

_____

2. Job's request is based on certain convictions about God and himself—convictions that his experiences have strained but not broken. What does Job say in the following passages?

13:15-19 _____

_____

_____

_____

_____

23:3-7 _____

_____

_____

_____

_____

_____

_____

For Thought and Discussion: What do you learn about Job's faith from the fact that he swears by God "who has denied me justice" (27:2) in an oath that is meant to invite God's judgment?

27:5-6 _____

_____

_____

_____

_____

As surely as God lives (27:2). Job's words are full of legal terminology. He desires to face God in court and be allowed to defend his own innocence. He also solemnly swears that he is innocent, using the formal oath of Israel's legal system. When a man was on trial in Israel and could not prove his innocence with evidence or witnesses, as a last resort he could take an oath inviting God to punish him if he was guilty. Theoretically, the human court would suspend judgment and await the divine verdict; either disaster would fall on the accused, or it would not. This provision protected people from false witnesses and imperfect methods of gathering evidence.

In 27:1-6, Job swears by the life of God Himself that he is not guilty, thereby setting himself beyond the judgment of his friends and inviting God to vindicate him. In his closing speech, 29:1–31:40, Job summarizes his evidence and ends with a long oath (see 31:5-40): "If I have . . . then let . . ." Faced with such a solemn invitation to be cursed if he is false, Job's friends can say nothing more (see 32:1).[2]

For Thought and Discussion: Job 27:11-23 is Job's words, not his friends'. What does Job believe about God? Are these words surprising on his lips? Why or why not?

3. Why does Job appeal to God for justice rather than to men (see 12:4-5; 13:3-12; 17:4,12; 26:1-4; 27:1-6)?

_____

_____

_____

_____

_____

_____

4. Chapters 39–31 are Job's final evidence, the case he would like to present to God. Read these chapters. What evidence does he state in his own defense (see 29:12-17; 31:4-40)?

_____

_____

_____

_____

_____

_____

_____

_____

5. Job knows that his only hope for justice is in God. However, the prospect of facing God in court terrifies him. Why is Job afraid to confront God, even though he longs to do so (see 9:2-20,28-32)?

_____

_____

**Optional
Application:** Could
you honestly claim
what Job claims in
29:12-17 and 31:4-40?
Look at those verses
for areas in which you
should change your
habits and priorities.
Do you find anything
on which you should
take action this week?

_____

_____

_____

_____

_____

6. Because Job both craves and dreads meeting
   God, what does he wish for, and indeed firmly
   believe he will get?

   9:33-35 _____

   _____

   _____

   _____

   16:18-21 _____

   _____

   _____

   _____

   19:23-27 _____

   _____

   _____

   _____

   _____

Mediate between us (9:33). "The Hebrew word
   mokih ["umpire" in NASB, RSV] does not mean a
   judge, who merely decides who is in the right;
   he is a mediator who settles the quarrel by rec-
   onciliation, a negotiator who brings both parties
   together, by laying *his hand upon us both* as
   a common friend." Job is not thinking of some

For Further Study:
Look up other references to the *go'el* — Psalm 19:14; 78:35; Proverbs 23:10-11; Isaiah 41:14; 43:14; 44:24; 63:16; Jeremiah 50:34.

For Thought and Discussion: In 19:25-27, Job emphasizes "I" and seeing with his own eyes. What does this tell you about his beliefs?

For Thought and Discussion: Most people of Job's day believed that death is the end for a man, as Job expresses in 14:7-12,18-22. How is Job different (see 14:13-17; 19:26-27)?

power greater than God who could "impose his authority on us both."[3]

Redeemer (19:25). The verb *gl* means "to redeem" or "to act as a kinsman." The noun *go'el* means "kinsman" and implies the duties that go with blood relationship. "The kinsman-redeemer was responsible for protecting the interests of needy members of the extended family — e.g., to provide an heir for a brother who had died (Deuteronomy 25:5-10), to redeem land that a poor relative had sold outside the family (Leviticus 25:25-28), to redeem a relative who had been sold into slavery [for debts] (see Leviticus 25:47-49) and to avenge the killing of a relative (Numbers 35:19-21; 'avenger' and 'kinsman-redeemer' are translations of the same Hebrew word)."[4]

So when Job says that he knows his *go'el* lives, he means he is sure that some brother or close kin will arise to defend his cause and save him from his afflictions. Clearly, this can't be a human blood relative. The Babylonians believed in minor gods such as guardian angels that stood up for people in the court of the great gods.[5] Elihu seems to believe in such guardians (see 33:23-25), but Eliphaz rejects the idea (see 4:18; 5:1; 15:15), and Job never speaks of angels at all. Job wants a *go'el* — a kinsman-redeemer.

In my flesh (19:26). The text of 19:23-27 is so garbled that translators have had headaches translating it. (You can tell this from the differences between versions and the number of footnotes in modern versions.) The NIV prefers "in my flesh" to "apart from my flesh" probably both because of New Testament teaching on bodily resurrection and because Job keeps talking about seeing with his eyes.

7. Job's arbiter or vindicator cannot be greater than God, for Job knows that no one can be (see 23:13). Ultimately, Job relies on God for vindication (see 17:3; 19:26-27; 23:1-7). Therefore, Job desires a vindicator who is God and yet an arbiter between God and man, a witness in heaven, an intercessor with God. What do Romans 5:1-2, 1 Timothy 2:5-6,

and Hebrews 4:14-16 say about this that Job doesn't know?

_____

_____

_____

_____

_____

For Thought and Discussion: Could one of the angels be Job's mediator? Why or why not? What do the friends think (see 4:18; 5:1; 15:15; 33:23-26)? What do you think, and why?

For Thought and Discussion: From the passages in this lesson, do you think Job is a good or poor example of faith in God? Why?

For Thought and Discussion: Does Job do what James 1:5-8 instructs us to do? Or is he a double-minded man? Support your opinion with passages from Job.

8. In 1 John 2:1-2, Jesus is described as the Advocate who speaks in our defense before the Father. Jesus' defense is that we are guilty but covered by His sacrifice for sin. How is this different from what Job wanted?

_____

_____

_____

_____

_____

9. Job's friends assume that he is suffering for some terrible crime. Therefore, his prayers—claims of innocence, requests for a trial and vindication, and desire for an arbiter (no begging for forgiveness)—all seem the height of arrogance (see 15:1-13; 18:1-4). Do you think Job is arrogant to demand a trial and an arbiter? Why or why not?

_____

_____

_____

_____

_____

_____

_____

Your response

10. Is there anything in this lesson that you want to take to heart this week? If so, what is it?

   _____

   _____

   _____

   _____

   _____

   _____

11. How do you see this truth already at work in your life?

   _____

   _____

   _____

   _____

   _____

12. How would you like this truth to affect what you do and think in deeper ways?

   _____

   _____

   _____

   _____

   _____

13. What can you do to cooperate with God in accomplishing this?

   _____

   _____

   _____

   _____

_____

_____

14. List any questions you have about this lesson.

_____

_____

_____

_____

For the group

Warm-up. Ask, "If you could meet God face-to-face today and tell Him exactly what you think of the way He is running the universe and your life, what would you say?" Encourage honesty. Some people might feel like Job, while others might feel very different.

Worship. Praise God for providing you with a mediator between Him and you. Thank Him that you are free to bring any fears, complaints, and requests to Him and that you will be heard and judged fairly. Bring anything on your heart to God.

1. Francis I. Andersen, _Job: An Introduction and Commentary_ (Downers Grove, IL: InterVarsity, 1984), 184.
2. Andersen, 220.
3. Andersen, 151.
4. Kenneth Barker, ed., _The NIV Study Bible_ (Grand Rapids, MI: Zondervan, 1985), 367. See also Roland de Vaux, _Ancient Israel: Volume 1: Social Institutions_ (New York: McGraw-Hill, 1961), 21–22.
5. Marvin Pope, _Job: Introduction, Translation, and Notes_ (Garden City, NY: Doubleday, 1973), 146.

Lesson Nine

JOB 3:1–37:24

What Is Man?

What is mankind that you make so much of them,
that you give them so much attention,
that you examine them every morning
and test them every moment? . . .
You will call and I will answer you;
you will long for the creature
your hands have made.
(Job 7:17-18; 14:15)

The debate between Job and his friends centers
around the nature and character of God—whether
He is truly just, good, and sovereign. But equally
important are questions about man: What does
God expect of a person? What kind of relationship
does God desire with a human, and how can it be
achieved? Without the fuller information that the
New Testament reveals, Job and his friends are
largely in the dark. Still, their questions are worth
wrestling with.

1. Job's friends think he has no right to question
   what God has done to him. What reasons do
   they give in the following passages? (What do
   they say about man and God?)

   4:17-21 _____

   _____

   _____

   _____

_____

_____

15:14-16 _____

_____

_____

_____

_____

25:1-6 _____

_____

_____

_____

_____

2. Job agrees that a man cannot possibly be righteous before God (see 9:2). But if this is true, says Job, something is wrong with his friends' counsel. What is wrong with what Bildad says in 8:6?

_____

_____

_____

_____

3. Job also agrees that man is an insignificant creature when compared to the Creator God. However, since this is so, what does Job find incomprehensible (see 7:17-21)?

_____

_____

_____

_____

4. Does God really consider man a "maggot" and "worm" (25:6)?

   a. What does Job think (see 10:8-12)?

   _____

   _____

   _____

   _____

   _____

   b. What does the rest of Scripture say?

   Genesis 1:26-31 _____

   _____

   _____

   _____

   _____

   _____

   Genesis 6:5-6; 8:21 _____

   _____

   _____

   _____

   Psalm 8:3-8 _____

   _____

   _____

   _____

   _____

   _____

   Luke 12:6-7,24-28 _____

   _____

   _____

For Thought and Discussion: Does it exalt God to call man "a maggot" (25:6)? Why or why not?

_____

_____

John 3:16 _____

_____

_____

_____

_____

5. Job's friends make a further deduction from God's greatness and man's smallness. What do Eliphaz and Elihu say?

22:3 _____

_____

_____

_____

35:6-8 _____

_____

_____

_____

6. Do you think these men are correct? Why or why not? (See Job 1:8; Isaiah 53:4-6; Luke 13:34; 19:41; 1 John 4:8-10.)

_____

_____

_____

_____

_____

_____

_____

_____

7. Job struggles with the fact that God requires people to be righteous even though total righteousness is impossible (see Job 9:2). If even a man like Job falls short, is God unfair to demand righteousness? Should a person despair? What answer does the New Testament give? (See Romans 3:20-26; 8:1-4; Philippians 2:12-13; John 15:1-5.)

For Further Study: What does your knowledge of Scripture lead you to think an ideal relationship with God should be like? (If you don't know, research this in the New Testament.) How can this be obtained?

_____

_____

_____

_____

_____

_____

_____

8. Job and his friends differ fundamentally over the kind of relationship they want to have with God. Job talks to God; they talk about Him. They want God to obey their system of blessing the righteous and punishing the wicked. What does Job want?

14:15 _____

_____

_____

19:26-27 _____

_____

_____

_____

_____

29:1-6 _____

_____

Optional Application: What does God think of you? What does He want your relationship with Him to be like? How will this affect your priorities this week?

_____
_____
_____
_____

9. Is Job's desired relationship superior or inferior to the one his friends want to have with God? Why?

_____
_____
_____
_____
_____
_____

Your response

10. What one insight from this lesson would you like to concentrate on for application this week? How do you want it to affect your life?

_____
_____
_____
_____
_____
_____
_____

11. What do you plan to do to take this insight to heart?

_____
_____

_____

_____

_____

12. List any questions you have about this lesson.

_____

_____

_____

_____

_____

Optional Application: Choose some verses from this lesson to memorize and meditate on this week.

For the group

Warm-up. Ask one or two people to describe the relationship they would like to have with God. Let them interpret the question as they like. Sharing this can help you understand each other better. Wait to evaluate how biblical your answers are until after you have discussed the lesson questions.

Summarize.

Questions. This lesson examines how Job and his friends think God views man and how biblically accurate their opinions are. After you've discussed questions 1 through 8, question 9 leads you back to the warm-up question. Compare the relationship with God you each think is desirable to what Job and his friends each seem to think is best. If you think the group needs a more biblical perspective, you can read and discuss John 15:1-17, Romans 8:15-17, Hebrews 4:14-16, Hebrews 10:19-23, or other passages you think are appropriate.

As always, be sure to save time to share how each of you wants to take personally the insights you have gained.

Wrap-up.

Worship. Thank God for what He thinks of you, for the relationship He desires to have with you, and for the lengths to which He has gone to achieve that relationship. Praise Him for His greatness compared to you and for the ways He cherishes you anyway.

JOB 28:1-28

The Fear of the Lord

The fear of the Lord—that is wisdom,
and to shun evil is understanding.
(Job 28:28)

The dialogue between Job and his three friends ends in a stalemate in chapter 27. Bildad's last speech is terse (see 25:1-6), as though he sees no reason to go on, and Zophar doesn't even bother to speak in the third round. Job has failed to convince the sages of his innocence, and they have failed to persuade him to repent. There is nothing more to be said.

Chapter 29 begins the three monologues on the case of Job versus God: Job sums up his argument and swears out an appeal to divine justice (see 29:1–31:40); Elihu declares the human verdict to testify, cross-examine, and state His verdict (see 38:1–41:34).

Between the dialogue in chapters 3–27 and the monologues in chapters 29–41, chapter 28 stands as an interlude and comment by the author. In this lesson, you'll take a look at that interlude to observe how its message is reflected in the rest of the book and to see how it applies to you. First read through 28:1-28.

It cannot be found in the land of the living
(28:13). This doesn't mean that no one on earth is capable of attaining wisdom (this would

contradict 28:28 and many of the psalms and proverbs). Rather, it means that wisdom cannot be obtained from the world. In particular, it cannot be gotten from the primeval powers of nature, Tehom (*the deep*) and Yam (*the sea*) named in 28:14. Nor can it be bought with money (see 28:15).[1]

1. What does the author think of man's technical ingenuity for acquiring precious minerals (see 28:1-11)?

_____

_____

_____

_____

_____

2. Why can't man use the same ingenuity to acquire wisdom (see 28:12-22)?

_____

_____

_____

_____

_____

_____

3. Therefore, to gain wisdom, what must a person do instead (see 28:23-28)?

_____

_____

_____

_____

_____

_____

4. Make up your own titles for chapter 28 and its three sections. Try to show the message of the chapter.

28:1-28 _____

_____

28:1-11 _____

_____

28:12-19 _____

_____

28:20-28 _____

_____

5. What does it mean to fear God? What insights do the following cross-references offer?

Psalm 112:1 _____

_____

_____

Psalm 139:1-10 _____

_____

_____

_____

_____

_____

Proverbs 3:7 _____

_____

_____

Isaiah 8:12-14 _____

_____

_____

_____

For Thought and Discussion: Why should people fear God?

Optional Application: Do you fear God? What evidence does your life give? How can you develop more fear of God and more of the character that goes with it?

For Thought and Discussion: Who claim to be wise in the book of Job (see 5:27; 8:8-10; 15:1-10)? Are they wise? How can you tell?

For Further Study: Find a definition of fearing God in a Bible dictionary.

Acts 10:2,35 _____

_____

_____

2 Corinthians 5:9-10 _____

_____

_____

6. From the passages in question 5, write out your own definition of fearing God.

_____

_____

_____

_____

_____

7. In 31:1-40, Job takes a solemn oath that he has shown fear of God in his life. Read 1:5,20-22; 2:3,10; 9:1-20; 19:23-27; 29:12-17; 30:25; 31:1-40. Write down everything Job has done to show either fear of God or lack of fear.

_____

_____

_____

_____

_____

_____

_____

_____

_____

_____

_____

_____

_____

_____

_____

For Thought and Discussion: Does 1 John 4:16-18 contradict Luke 12:4-5 and Job 28:28? Explain why or why not. Take the context of each passage into account.

8. From the definition in 28:28, which of the characters in the book of Job do you think is a wise man, and how can you tell?

For Thought and Discussion: Does Job do what you listed in question 7 to try to earn God's favor? How can you tell? Why is this important?

_____

_____

_____

_____

_____

Your response

9. Should Christians fear God and shun evil, or has faith in Jesus replaced this as a means to wisdom? Why or why not? (Support your view with Scripture, such as Matthew 22:34-40; Luke 12:4-5; 1 Peter 2:17; Revelation 14:7; 15:4.)

_____

_____

_____

_____

10. What one insight from this lesson would you like to apply to your own life?

_____

_____

Optional Application: Are you committed to seeking wisdom, or do you trust in human ingenuity and intelligence? Pray about this.

Optional Application: Choose one practice of Job's that you listed in question 7, one that you would like to make your own habit. Write it down and describe how you fall short in this area. Talk with God about what you can do to acquire this habit.

_____

_____

_____

11. How do you fall short or want to change with regard to this insight?

_____

_____

_____

_____

_____

12. What action and prayer can you pursue this week to apply this truth?

_____

_____

_____

_____

_____

_____

13. List any questions you have about this lesson.

_____

_____

_____

_____

For the group

Warm-up. Ask what the group thinks it means to fear God. Later, when you discuss questions 5 through 7, you can refine your definitions with examples in Job and cross-references from the New Testament.

Read aloud and summarize. Have someone use question 4 to summarize what chapter 28 of Job is about.

Questions. Spend the bulk of your time discussing what it means to fear God, whether Christians should do it and why, and how you can act on what you have learned. Many people feel that because "perfect love drives out fear" (1 John 4:18), we should not fear God as Old Testament people did. Because of this belief, you should carefully define how wise fear and faithless fear of God are different.

Worship. Praise God for being the One who alone knows and reveals the way to wisdom. Worship Him with godly fear. Job 28:23-28 and Revelation 14:7, 15:3-4, and 19:5 may help you with worship. Ask God to teach you righteous fear of Him.

1. Francis I. Andersen, *Job: An Introduction and Commentary* (Downers Grove, IL: InterVarsity, 1984), 227.

JOB 38:1-40:5

Wisdom

Who has the wisdom to count the clouds?
(Job 38:37)

Job has been pleading for an audience with God, imploring God to break His terrifying silence. Job wants God to explain why He is doing inexplicable things, but Job will even be satisfied to answer questions if God will speak (see 13:22). The sages have been reduced to silence, Job has invoked divine judgment with a solemn oath of innocence, and Elihu has pronounced what he thinks is the last word. In the stillness a storm swells, and from it thunders the voice of the Lord.

1. Job's visitors think they understand God. Zophar is sure he knows what the Almighty will say if He comes (see 11:5-6). Imagine that, like them, you don't know what the Lord is going to say to Job. What would you expect Him to say?

   _____

   _____

   _____

   _____

   _____

2. Why would you expect this?

_____

_____

_____

_____

_____

_____

Keep your answers to questions 1 and 2 in mind as you study what God does in fact say to Job. Keep asking yourself, *Why is this a better answer to Job than what I would have expected?*

Would you discredit my justice? (40:8). As so often in Job, the key to God's speeches is in the middle of His words, not the beginning or the end. In Israel, being a judge meant two things: pronouncing the verdict and securing the right for the injured party. No matter how wise a person was in deciding cases, if he lacked the ability to enforce his decree, then he was useless as a judge.[1] Conversely, if he was powerful but not wise enough to discern all the implications of the case, then he could be a judge but not a good one.

In 38:1–41:34, God addresses both of these issues. In 38:1–40:2, His questions deal with wisdom, knowledge, and understanding. In 40:6–41:34, they deal with power.

---

3. The Lord's first speech is two sets of rhetorical questions. What does He ask Job about in . . .

38:4-38? _____

_____

_____

_____

_____

38:39–39:30? _____

_____

_____

_____

_____

_____

Obscures my plans (38:2). The Lord could be accusing Job of obscuring the divine design with muddled questions and accusations. However, this seems to contradict 42:7. So God could be saying that Job is darkening counsel (the advice of a wise man) because of his ignorance. Job has spoken truth (see 42:7), but severely limited truth.[2]

4. Nowhere does God accuse Job of any sin for which he is being punished. Why is this important?

_____

_____

_____

_____

_____

5. However, God does charge Job with speaking without knowledge (see 38:2). What sorts of ignorant things has Job been saying? (*Optional:* See 7:21; 9:14-20; 16:7-14; 19:6; 40:2,8.)

_____

_____

_____

_____

For Thought and Discussion: Why do you think the Lord doesn't shake the wicked out every morning (see 38:13)? What would happen to us if He did? What does this tell you about His character and purposes?

6. Knowledge, wisdom, and understanding are crucial qualifications for one who would be the judge of the universe. What crucial knowledge does Job lack that would enable him to be the judge and evaluate God's ways? (Consider 1:1–2:6; 38:1–39:30.)

_____

_____

_____

_____

_____

_____

_____

7. Does God have enough wisdom to run the universe? What evidence does He present in 38:4–39:30?

_____

_____

_____

_____

_____

_____

Shake the wicked (38:13). God describes the dawn as shaking the earth like a blanket to rid it of vermin. But the Judge of the universe does not do this each morning. In accord with His mysterious wisdom, He leaves the wicked in the world.

8. Some people think God's questions are harshly sarcastic and angry, while others think His sarcasm is good-humored jibing between friends. Still others find no humor or sarcasm in God's words, only majestic seriousness. What do you think God's attitude toward Job is in 38:1–39:30, and why?

_____

_____

_____

_____

_____

_____

_____

9. a. Does God treat Job like a worm (see 25:6)? How does He treat him (see 38:3)?

_____

_____

_____

b. How is this significant for you personally?

_____

_____

_____

_____

_____

10. Because of his suffering, Job began to wonder about God's goodness (see 23:13–24:25). What evidence of God's goodness or lack of it do you see in 38:1–39:30?

_____

_____

For Thought and Discussion: a. God waters the wastelands where humans don't live (see 38:25-27). He makes creatures like the lion, wild ass, and wild ox, which are useless to man (see 38:38-41; 39:5-12). What can we conclude about God's interests from these actions? What do these works tell you about Him?

b. Think about some of the other things God has made: snow, lightning, stars, the ostrich, and so on (see 38:22-24,31-32; 39:13-18). What do these reveal about Him?

c. Does everything in the world focus on man? What does 38:1–39:30 say?

103

For Thought and Discussion: Would you be satisfied that God is good if you were Job hearing 38:1–39:30? Why or why not?

_____

_____

_____

_____

11. What would you answer to any of God's questions in 38:2–39:30? How would you feel about yourself and God if He addressed these questions to you?

_____

_____

_____

_____

_____

12. How does Job respond to God's questions (see 40:3-5)? What do his words mean?

_____

_____

_____

_____

13. Now that you've examined the *content* and the *effect* of God's questions, why do you think He answered Job with questions, particularly these questions?

_____

_____

_____

_____

Your response

For Thought and Discussion: Was Job wrong to question God? Why or why not?

14. Examine your own circumstances and feelings about God in light of 38:1–39:30. How are God's words relevant to you?

_____

_____

_____

_____

_____

15. How would you like to respond to God's words in prayer and/or action this week? What habits or attitudes would you like to change or develop, and how can you begin doing this with God's help?

_____

_____

_____

_____

_____

_____

16. List any questions you have about this lesson.

_____

_____

_____

_____

For the group

Warm-up. Questions 1 and 2 are excellent warm-ups, and you should ask group members to share their answers before reading 38:1–40:5. We know that what God *does* say is ultimately what He *should* say (because God is always right), but we can learn about ourselves and our deep beliefs from what we expect or want God to say. Don't take time to debate how valid or biblical your gut feelings and expectations are; just share them and move on. Be prepared for some answers that you find crazy. You'll want to spend most of your time discussing *what* God does say and *why* that is the best possible answer to Job.

Read aloud. The tone of voice with which you read God's questions reveals much about how you interpret them. Should you be sarcastic? Gentle? Angry? Patient? Haughty? When you choose someone to read 38:1–40:5, ask him or her to think about the proper tone of voice before beginning to read. Better still, divide the passage among several readers, and ask each to use what he or she thinks is the appropriate tone.

Summarize.

Questions. Ask if the group was surprised by God's response to Job, and why or why not. Then go on with whichever numbered and optional questions you have chosen.

Worship. Praise God for all His wisdom and understanding revealed in 38:1–39:30. Praise Him for the specific things that impress each of you. Thank Him that you can rely on His wisdom to run the universe.

1. Francis I. Andersen, *Job: An Introduction and Commentary* (Downers Grove, IL: InterVarsity, 1984), 286.
2. Andersen, 273–274; Kenneth Barker, ed., *The NIV Study Bible* (Grand Rapids, MI: Zondervan, 1985), 775.

JOB 40:6-42:6

An Arm Like God's

Do you have an arm like God's,
and can your voice thunder like his?
Then adorn yourself with glory and splendor,
and clothe yourself in honor and majesty. . . .
Then I myself will admit to you
that your own right hand can save you.
(Job 40:9-10,14)

In 38:1–39:30, the Lord displayed His wisdom. He, not Job, made and understands the earth, the sea, light and darkness, snow and rain, the mountain goat and the hawk. He made the animals and the weather to delight Himself, and man is only one part of His glorious universe. But although beholding God's wisdom has reduced Job to silence (see 40:3-5), it has not fully satisfied him, so God asks another round of questions. Read 40:6–42:6.

Behemoth (40:15). This Hebrew word means "beasts," implying that this is the beast of beasts, the fiercest of the land animals. Some interpreters think the fanciful language (such as 40:18) suggests a mythological or super-natural creature. Others note that God calls the behemoth a creature like Job (see 40:15) and that God uses poetic imagery to describe many natural works ("water jars of the heavens" for rain in 38:37). In this case, "behemoth" may refer to some huge animal, such as the hippo-potamus or elephant.[1]

Leviathan (41:1). In Canaanite and other ancient myths, this is the seven-headed sea serpent that the god Baal must battle and defeat. However, God may be using this familiar name for a real sea animal, such as the crocodile.[2]

1. A judge must be not only wise enough to decide what is right but also powerful enough to see that right prevails. What must the Judge of the universe be able to do?

    40:9-14 _____

    _____

    _____

    _____

    _____

    40:15-24 _____

    _____

    _____

    _____

    41:1-34 _____

    _____

    _____

    _____

    _____

2. How does Job measure up on this scale?

    _____

    _____

    _____

    _____

    _____

AN ARM LIKE GOD'S

3. What impressions do you get of God from
   40:9–41:34?

   _____

   _____

   _____

   _____

   _____

4. Job's friends thought they knew how to
   manage God: Be good and all will be well. How
   manageable does God sound to you in 40:9–
   41:34? Why do you think so?

   _____

   _____

   _____

   _____

   _____

Dust and ashes (42:6). These symbolized humilia-
   tion and lowliness (compare Genesis 18:27).[3]

5. How does Job respond to God's second set of
   questions (see 42:1-6)?

   _____

   _____

   _____

   _____

   _____

6. Consider 2:3-6 and 42:2-3,7. What do you
   think Job is repenting of in 42:6? (Is he finally
   agreeing with his visitors that his suffering has

For Further Study:
Does Isaiah 55:8-9 express some of what God is getting at in Job 40:6–41:34? Explain.

been punishment for unrepented sin, or is he repenting for something else?)

_____

_____

_____

_____

_____

_____

7. When Eliphaz and Elihu spoke about God's greatness, Job was unmoved. He knew God was powerful; it was His goodness as a ruler that Job wondered about. Why doesn't Job doubt God anymore (see 42:5)?

_____

_____

_____

_____

_____

8. Job's attitudes toward God and life are radically changed not by hearing about God nor by having his sickness healed and property restored but by _seeing_ God (see 42:5). Why do you think this makes the difference?

_____

_____

_____

_____

_____

_____

9. How can we get beyond just hearing or reading about God to know Him as Job has come to know Him? (Should we ask God to appear out of a storm?)

_____

_____

_____

_____

_____

_____

For Thought and Discussion: In your opinion, why didn't God answer Job's questions or explain about Satan and the test? What does this reveal about God?

10. Did God answer Job's questions? If so, how? If not, why was Job finally satisfied? (Recall from 13:20-22; 19:7; and 30:20 what Job wanted, and compare these verses to 42:5.)

_____

_____

_____

_____

_____

11. If you were in Job's circumstances, would 38:1–41:34 satisfy you? Why or why not?

_____

_____

_____

_____

_____

_____

Your response

12. How is 40:6–42:6 relevant to your life? What insights would you like to take to heart?

_____

_____

_____

_____

_____

_____

13. Is there any response you plan to make to these passages? If so, write it down.

_____

_____

_____

_____

_____

14. List any questions you have about 40:6–42:6.

_____

_____

_____

_____

For the group

Warm-up. Ask group members how they have seen God at work during the past week.

Read aloud.

Questions. This section has puzzled readers for centuries. Why does God's outpouring of seemingly sarcastic rhetorical questions satisfy Job? There are cross-references that definitively answer this, so you will have to use your brains, what you know about God and Job, and your own experiences. You can also look at some of the solutions commentators have offered. Be sure to discuss what differences all this should make to your lives.

Worship. Spend time worshipping the God who made the behemoth and rules the leviathan. Ask Him to help you get beyond hearing about Him to beholding Him.

1. Francis I. Andersen, *Job: An Introduction and Commentary* (Downers Grove, IL: InterVarsity, 1984), 288–289; Kenneth Barker, ed., *The NIV Study Bible* (Grand Rapids, MI: Zondervan, 1985), 778.
2. Andersen, 289–290; Barker, 778–779.
3. Andersen, 292; Barker, 765, 779.

Lesson Thirteen

JOB 42:7-17 AND REVIEW

Epilogue

You have not spoken the truth about me,
as my servant Job has.
(Job 42:7-8)

Job is satisfied just by seeing and hearing God. But the Lord has some loose ends to tie up, now that Job's test is over. Read 42:7-17.

The references in questions 1, 2, 5, and 6 are intended to help you find questions and passages you discussed weeks ago. Use them as you like; don't feel you must read all of them if your time is limited.

1. The Lord is angry with the sages because they "have not spoken of me what is right, as my servant Job has" (42:7-8). How have they not spoken rightly about God? (See your answers to questions 1 through 4 and 7 and 8 of lesson 4, questions 1 and 2 and 10 and 11 of lesson 5, questions 1 and 2 of lesson 6, question 6 of lesson 7, and question 5 of lesson 9. *Optional:* See parts of 4:1–5:27; 8:1-22; 11:1-20; 13:7-12; 15:1-16; 22:1-30.)

_____

_____

_____

_____

_____

For Thought and Discussion: a. To restore relationship between God and Job, all that was necessary was meeting and talking. What did the sages have to do that Job didn't (see 42:8)?

b. Why was this necessary for them and not for him?

For Thought and Discussion: Does the "happy ending" of Job seem satisfying or unnatural to you? Does it fulfill or ruin the story for you? Why do you feel that way?

For Further Study:
Compare Job 42:8-9
to Matthew 5:44. How
does Job exemplify
Jesus' teaching?

**For Thought and
Discussion:** Does
God always restore
what He takes away?
Why or why not?

2. God rebuked Job for speaking ignorantly about
Him (see 38:2; 40:2,8). Nevertheless, how has
Job spoken what is right about God? (Consider
your answers to questions 4 and 7 of lesson 2;
questions 2 through 7 of lesson 3; questions 2,
5, 6, 8, and 9 of lesson 5; questions 3, 5, 6, and
8 of lesson 6; questions 1, 2, and 4 of lesson
7; questions 1, 2, 3, 5, and 6 of lesson 8; and
questions 4, 8, and 9 of lesson 9. *Optional:* See
parts of 1:21; 2:10; 9:1–10:22; 12:1-25; 13:13-28;
14:13-22; 16:6-21; 19:1-29; 21:1-34; 23:1–24:25;
27:1-6; 29:1–31:40.)

3. What else did God do for Job besides appearing
and speaking to him (see 42:10-17)?

4. Did God have to do all this? Do you think He would have been unjust if He hadn't? Why or why not?

_____

_____

_____

_____

_____

For Thought and Discussion: a. What are some possible reasons for suffering? (See question 8 of lesson 7.)

b. Do we need to know why we are suffering? Why or why not?

For Thought and Discussion: Is it okay to question God? Why or why not?

Review

If the book of Job seems a jumble of details to you now, a review can help you pull the threads together. If you have time, consider taking an extra week to get all the way through this review. Alternatively, you can omit some questions. Again, don't feel you must look at all the references; they are only suggestions.

5. Describe God as the book of Job reveals Him. (*Optional:* See 1:6–2:6; 9:1-13; 10:1-22; 12:13-35; 14:13-22; 21:17-26; 23:1-17; 26:6-14; 36:22–42:17.)

_____

_____

_____

_____

_____

_____

6. How did Job relate to God? (*Optional:* See 1:21; 2:10; 13:15; 14:14-17; 19:23-27; 21:4; 23:1-7; 28:28; 29:1-6; 30:20.)

_____

_____

For Thought and Discussion: Why should we love God?

For Thought and Discussion: James 5:11 says that Job's perseverance is a model for us. How did Job show perseverance?

7. To what extent do you think Job's way of relating to God is a model we should follow, and to what extent is it not? Explain your reasons for your view.

_____

_____

_____

_____

_____

_____

8. Job was tested to prove whether he loved and respected God (a) only as long as it was profitable for him to do so, or (b) because God was inherently worthy. Which turned out to be true? How can you tell?

_____

_____

_____

_____

_____

_____

9. What have you learned from the book of Job about . . .

faith? _____

_____

_____

_____

_____

how to deal with suffering? _____

_____

_____

_____

_____

10. Did you learn any other important things from Job? If so, write them down to remember them.

_____

_____

_____

_____

_____

11. At the end of lessons 1 through 12, you wrote questions you had about the book. Do any remain unanswered? If so, record them here and plan ways to get answers. You can consult some of the references on pages 123–125 or ask someone whose biblical knowledge you trust.

_____

_____

_____

_____

_____

_____

12. How have you changed (attitudes, beliefs, habits, priorities) as a result of studying Job?

_____

_____

_____

_____

_____

_____

13. Look back at questions in which you expressed a desire to make some application. Are you satisfied with your follow-through? If there are any areas you would still like to work on, jot them here along with any plans you have for prayer or action.

_____

_____

_____

_____

_____

_____

_____

For the group

Warm-up. Ask, "Does anyone here feel that God has taken away from you someone or something very important to you?" Give everyone a minute to think, and then ask, "What would have to happen for you to feel satisfied that God has treated you justly and lovingly?" Give everyone who wants one a chance to answer.

Read aloud. Read 42:7-17.

Epilogue. Questions 1 and 2 offer lots of references so as not to limit your answers. If your group is likely to find so much of the book overwhelming, you can assign each person to examine one or two of the passages in each question. Then you can pool your observations. Alternatively, you can take a whole meeting to cover questions 1 through 4, and a second one for your review.

Review. You may want to take another meeting to finish this review or select one or two questions that are most relevant to your group. Be sure to allow time for questions 11 through 13.

Evaluation. Take a few minutes or a whole other meeting to evaluate how well your group functioned during your study of Job. Some questions you might ask are:

> What did you learn about small-group study?
> How well did your study help you grasp the book of Job?
> What did you like least? What would you change?
> How well did you meet the goals you set at your first meeting?
> What are members' current needs? What will you do next?

Worship. Praise God for everything He has taught you through Job. Ask Him to continue to reveal Himself.

STUDY AIDS

For further information on the material in this study, consider the following sources. They are available on the Internet (www.christianbook.com, www.amazon.com, etc.), or your local Christian bookstore should be able to order any of them if it does not carry them. Most seminary libraries have them, as well as many university and public libraries.

Commentaries on Job

Anders, Max, ed. *Job, Holman Old Testament Commentary Volume 10* (B&H Publishing Company, 2005).
    Great resource for lay teachers and pastors alike. This verse-by-verse commentary illuminates the connection between various passages within Job and other parts of Scripture. Includes discussion starters, teaching plans, and more.

Janzen, J. Gerald. *Job, Interpretation Commentary* (Westminster, John Knox Press, 1985).
    This serious commentary provides good exegetical tools for teaching and preaching. Includes synopsis of text, along with thoughtful discussion of historical, cultural, literary, and linguistic issues. Especially good in its treatment of Yahweh's speeches and Job's responses in Job 42.

Stedman, Ray C. *Let God Be God* (Discovery House, 2007).
    Who knew a book about Job could be warm, humorous, and encouraging? But this one is. Wonderful insights into the nature of suffering, the character of God, the reality of humanity, and encouragement that can be found even in the midst of trials when we understand things through God's perspective.

Historical background sources and handbooks

Bible study becomes more meaningful when modern Western readers understand the times and places in which the biblical authors lived. *The IVP Bible
Background Commentary: Old Testament*, by John H. Walton, Victor H.
Matthews, and Mark Chavalas (InterVarsity, 2000), provides insight into the
ancient Near Eastern world, its peoples, customs, and geography, to help con-
temporary readers better understand the context in which the Old Testament
Scriptures were written.

A *handbook* of biblical customs can also be useful. Some good ones
are the time-proven updated classic, *Halley's Bible Handbook with the New
International Version*, by Henry H. Halley (Zondervan, 2007), and the inex-
pensive paperback *Manners and Customs in the Bible*, by Victor H. Matthews
(Hendrickson, 1991).

Concordances, dictionaries, and encyclopedias

A *concordance* lists words of the Bible alphabetically along with each verse in
which the word appears. It lets you do your own word studies. An *exhaustive*
concordance lists every word used in a given translation, while an *abridged*
or *complete* concordance omits either some words, some occurrences of the
word, or both.

Two of the best exhaustive concordances are *Strong's Exhaustive
Concordance* and *The Strongest NIV Exhaustive Concordance*. *Strong's* is
available based on the King James Version of the Bible and the New American
Standard Bible. *Strong's* has an index by which you can find out which Greek
or Hebrew word is used in a given English verse. The NIV concordance does
the same thing except it also includes an index for Aramaic words in the original texts from which the NIV was translated. However, neither concordance
requires knowledge of the original languages. *Strong's* is available online at
www.biblestudytools.com. Both are also available in hard copy.

A *Bible dictionary* or *Bible encyclopedia* alphabetically lists articles about
people, places, doctrines, important words, customs, and geography of the Bible.

Holman Illustrated Bible Dictionary, by C. Brand, C. W. Draper, and A.
England (B&H, 2003), offers more than seven hundred color photos, illustrations, and charts; sixty full-color maps; and up-to-date archeological findings;
along with exhaustive definitions of people, places, things, and events — deal-
ing with every subject in the Bible. It uses a variety of Bible translations and is
the only dictionary that includes the HCSB, NIV, KJV, RSV, NRSV, REB, NASB, ESV, and
TEV.

The New Unger's Bible Dictionary, Revised and Expanded, by Merrill F.
Unger (Moody, 2006), has been a best seller for almost fifty years. Its 6,700-
plus entries reflect the most current scholarship and more than 1,200,000
words are supplemented with detailed essays, colorful photography and maps,
and dozens of charts and illustrations to enhance your understanding of
God's Word. Based on the New American Standard Version.

The Zondervan Encyclopedia of the Bible, edited by Moisés Silva and Merrill C. Tenney (Zondervan, 2008), is excellent and exhaustive. However, its five 1,000-page volumes are a financial investment, so all but very serious students may prefer to use it at a church, public, college, or seminary library.

Unlike a Bible dictionary in the above sense, *Vine's Complete Expository Dictionary of Old and New Testament Words,* by W. E. Vine, Merrill F. Unger, and William White Jr. (Thomas Nelson, 1996), alphabetically lists major words used in the King James Version and defines each Old Testament Hebrew or New Testament Greek word the KJV translates with that English word. *Vine's* lists verse references where that Hebrew or Greek word appears so that you can do your own cross-references and word studies without knowing the original languages.

The Brown-Driver-Briggs Hebrew and English Lexicon by Francis Brown, C. Briggs, and S. R. Driver (Hendrickson, 1996), is probably the most respected and comprehensive Bible lexicon for Old Testament studies. *BDB* gives not only dictionary definitions for each word but relates each word to its Old Testament usage and categorizes its nuances of meaning.

Bible atlases and map books

A *Bible atlas* can be a great aid to understanding what is going on in a book of the Bible and how geography affected events. Here are a few good choices:

The Hammond Atlas of Bible Lands (Langenscheidt, 2007) packs a ton of resources into just sixty-four pages. Maps, of course, but also photographs, illustrations, and a comprehensive timeline. Includes an introduction to the unique geography of the Holy Land, including terrain, trade routes, vegetation, and climate information.

The New Moody Atlas of the Bible, by Barry J. Beitzel (Moody, 2009), is scholarly, very evangelical, and full of theological text, indexes, and references. Beitzel shows vividly how God prepared the land of Israel perfectly for the acts of salvation He was going to accomplish in it.

Then and Now Bible Maps Insert (Rose, 2008) is a nifty paperback that is sized just right to fit inside your Bible cover. Only forty-four pages long, it features clear plastic overlays of modern-day cities and countries so you can see what nation or city now occupies the Bible setting you are reading about. Every major city of the Bible is included.

For small-group leaders

Discipleship Journal's Best Small-Group Ideas, Volumes 1 and 2 (NavPress, 2005).

Each volume is packed with 101 of the best hands-on tips and group-building principles from *Discipleship Journal's* "Small Group Letter" and "DJ Plus" as well as articles from the magazine. They will help you inject new passion into the life of your small group.

Donahue, Bill. *Leading Life-Changing Small Groups* (Zondervan, 2002).
     This comprehensive resource is packed with information, practical tips, and insights that will teach you about small-group philosophy and structure, discipleship, conducting meetings, and more.

McBride, Neal F. *How to Build a Small-Groups Ministry* (NavPress, 1994).
     How to Build a Small-Groups Ministry is a time-proven, hands-on workbook for pastors and lay leaders that includes everything you need to know to develop a plan that fits your unique church. Through basic principles, case studies, and worksheets, McBride leads you through twelve logical steps for organizing and administering a small-groups ministry.

McBride, Neal F. *How to Lead Small Groups* (NavPress, 1990).
     This book covers leadership skills for all kinds of small groups: Bible study, fellowship, task, and support groups. Filled with step-by-step guidance and practical exercises to help you grasp the critical aspects of small-group leadership and dynamics.

Miller, Tara, and Jenn Peppers. *Finding the Flow: A Guide for Leading Small Groups and Gatherings* (IVP Connect, 2008).
     Finding the Flow offers a fresh take on leading small groups by seeking to develop the leader's small-group facilitation skills.

Bible study methods

Discipleship Journal's Best Bible Study Methods (NavPress, 2002).
     This is a collection of thirty-two creative ways to explore Scripture that will help you enjoy studying God's Word more.

Hendricks, Howard, and William Hendricks. *Living by the Book: The Art and Science of Reading the Bible* (Moody, 2007).
     Living by the Book offers a practical three-step process that will help you master simple yet effective inductive methods of observation, interpretation, and application that will make all the difference in your time with God's Word. A workbook by the same title is also available to go along with the book.

The Navigator Bible Studies Handbook (NavPress, 1994).
     This resource teaches the underlying principles for doing good inductive Bible study, including instructions on doing queston-and-answer studies, verse-analysis studies, chapter-analysis studies, and topical studies.

Warren, Rick. *Rick Warren's Bible Study Methods: Twelve Ways You Can Unlock God's Word* (HarperCollins, 2006).
     Rick Warren offers simple, step-by-step instructions, guiding you through twelve different approaches to studying the Bible for yourself with the goal of becoming more like Jesus.

Encounter God's Word

EXPERIENCE LIFECHANGE

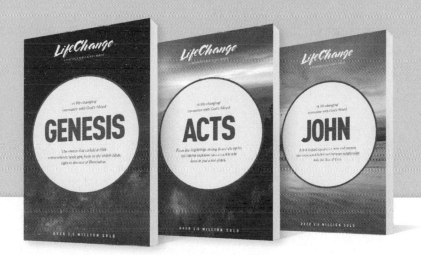